NEW CREATIONISM

NEW CREATIONISM

Harold Clark

Southern Publishing Association, Nashville, Tennessee

Copyright © 1980 by
Southern Publishing Association

This book was
Edited by Gerald Wheeler
Designed by Mark O'Connor
Cover design by Dean Tucker

Type set: 11/13 Palatino
Printed in U.S.A.

Library of Congress Cataloging in Publication Data

Clark, Harold Willard, 1891-
  The new creationism.

  Bibliography: pp. 124-126
  1. Creation.   2. Evolution.   3. Deluge.
I. Title.
BS651.C554   213   79-22250
ISBN 0-8127-0247-6 (Cloth Edition)

Contents

Preface

Today, as never before, the question of the origin of the earth and its life agitates the scientific world. Recent advances in natural history have thrown light on many problems relating to the distribution of plants and animals, influence of the environment, and the effect of natural forces on the lives of plants, animals, and man. New discoveries in genetics, particularly with respect to DNA, have given much information on the origin and transmission of hereditary characters. Ideas based on common sense and supported by experimental evidence have superseded superstitions hoary with age. In spite of much confusion in the public mind regarding the problem of the origin of species, the present situation is more favorable to a solution of the question than ever before, and the field of geology has thrown new light on what has produced fossils.

In spite of the advances in science, the relationship between science and religion still offers many perplexing questions. On one side we find extensive discussion purporting to prove that all changes in living things mean evolution. But on the other side we observe a growing body of scientific evidence indicating that the Genesis record of Creation and the Flood has much greater validity than we have generally recognized.

It might be well to state the author's fundamental philosophy so that the reader will know from what viewpoint he approaches the subject. Accordingly let me say that the basic assumptions behind this treatise are the following:

1. The Bible is the Inspired Word of God, and as such it must be accepted as authority on whatever matters it speaks.

2. The Genesis record of Creation and the early history of the world is not allegory or myth but an inspired historical account.

3. Any scientific theory regarding the origin of the earth and its life must agree with the plain, obvious rendering of the Genesis record.

This book is not for the scientist but for the layman. Nontechnical and nonargumentative, it presents the scientific data relating to the evolution-creation controversy in ordinary, everyday language so as to help the reader as far as possible to understand the evidence bearing on the subject.

A brief history of the development of current viewpoints comes first, after which the book considers the various problems. The author earnestly hopes that it will lead to a deeper and fuller appreciation of the perfect harmony between the book of revelation and the book of nature.

Harold W. Clark

Chapter 1

Conflict and Controversy

In the apostasy that arose after the Flood, humanity forgot the true God and attributed supernatural powers to all natural objects. Man regarded nature as self-operating and personified natural forces in terms of gods and goddesses. He conceived of gods of springtime, of storm, of harvest. In fact, he regarded every aspect of nature as having a deity within it.

About five hundred years before Christ, Greek scholars attempted to derive some order and system out of the jumble of superstition. They began to build a philosophy (Greek: *philos*, "loving"; *sophos*, "wisdom"—a love of knowledge). As they developed their idea, it was an attempt to understand rationally all of nature's activities, an approach sometimes known as naturalism because of trying to explain everything by natural causes.

The Greeks proposed various schemes. Some thought that fire was the source of all natural phenomena. Other philosophers attributed creative activity to water, and so on, without much success. Finally, about the middle of the fourth century BC, Aristotle, often considered the greatest thinker of all times, taught that nature possessed what he called an inherent perfecting tendency. It has within itself, he asserted, the power to progress from a simple, unorganized state to the highly complex condition of today. By this onward drive all forms of life have developed, and even the gods were merely men and women who had attained a higher state of existence.

For this perfecting tendency Aristotle coined the term "evolution," which means "an unrolling" or "expansion." His philosophy passed on to succeeding generations, and ever since his time has had a profound influence on philosophical and scientific thought. However, his theory was not the same as the modern theory of evolution.

In the early days Christians of our era made efforts to harmonize Greek thought with their own teachings, and much confusion resulted. During the fifth century Augustine, one of the outstanding theologians of all time, when dealing with the problem of Creation, declared that it would not be wise to antagonize the scientific men of the world by advocating narrow views. He therefore proposed that Creation was not a finished work but that God had created the world *in potentia*—that is, in a simple state and endowed with certain properties by which it would be able to develop from the primitive condition to the present complex state. Such a progression, of course, would take long ages of time.

Modern writers have characterized his viewpoint as a full-fledged theistic evolution, that is, evolution under the direction of God. Sometimes people speak of it as creation by means of evolution. It contradicts,

10

however, the literal interpretation of the Genesis record of Creation in six days.

Augustine's philosophy became the orthodox teaching of the church, and it remained so until the Reformation called men's attention back to the literal Bible record. Christians in many different churches still do accept it though.

After Islam had spread over the southern shores of the Mediterranean and into the Middle East, it set up universities from Baghdad in Mesopotamia to Cordova in Spain. Many European students attended them and carried back into Europe the knowledge they obtained. The Arabian universities developed Aristotle's philosophy, and doubtless their influence had much to do with the establishment of a scientific philosophy in Europe when that continent began to awaken from the slumber of the Dark Ages.

In the fourteenth century came the Renaissance, or revival of learning. The crusaders brought back with them books and manuscripts from the Arabian world, among them many of Aristotle's writings. Studied in the universities of Europe, Aristotle's works played a large part in molding the thought of the awakening modern world.

Thus, when the scientific period arose in Europe in the fifteenth and sixteenth centuries, the philosophic background of many students was that of Aristotle, whose ideas had come to them by way of three channels—the church, the Arabian universities, and directly from his own writings. As a result, when men began to investigate the formation of the rocks, they interpreted them in terms of long ages of time.

11

New Creationism

When the Reformation developed in the sixteenth century it emphasized the Bible as the only rule of faith, which had a tendency to hold back the wave of philosophic interpretation that had dominated the halls of learning. Most reformers held literally to the Genesis record of Creation and the Flood. At the same time the Catholic Counter-Reformation arose to meet the challenge of literal creationism taught by the Protestants. It also taught that the Genesis record was valid. For about three hundred years, in what some have called the golden age of creationism, both influences held men close to the Bible account.

As Europe began to emerge from the Dark Ages a great interest developed in the natural sciences. One science that the common people could easily study was botany, as wild flowers grew everywhere. Many made collections of them and attempted to name them. An English naturalist, John Ray (1627-1705), made one of the first successful classification schemes. His *General History of Plants*, published in London from 1686-1704, described 18,600 plants, all that were known to the botanists of Europe. He wrote also on animals.

The work of the Swedish botanist Carl von Linné—Charles Linnaeus as known in English—followed that of Ray. Linnaeus traveled widely over Europe, collecting and classifying plants. Appointed professor of natural history at the University of Uppsala, he trained students who explored a large part of the known world in search of new plants and animals. During 1735-1758 he published his *Systema Naturae*—"System of Nature." It became the starting point for the modern scientific plants and animals. He set up four categories of classification—class, order, genus, and species. Later, taxonomists inserted the family as a division of the order and added the highest category of all, the phylum. Scientists name a plant or animal by giving its genus and species name. For instance, Linnaeus named the common tea roses *Rosa indica* and the oxeye daisy, *Chrysanthemum leucanthemum*. The scientific world still uses the names—in fact, modern botanists still employ any name given by Linnaeus.

Linnaeus' ideas regarding the origin of species were not clear. In his early writings he asserted that he recognized as many species as there were different forms in the beginning. He did not believe that species could change. His concept became known as the doctrine of fixity of species. Later he recognized that some species had apparently been derived from others or had been variants from the original types.

During the century following Linnaeus the doctrine of fixity of species held a dominant place in the biological sciences. On the other hand, some of his contemporaries, particularly Georges Buffon, a great French naturalist, felt that the scholarly world should give more attention to variation. Buffon was not clear about how much variation he thought was possible, but some have regarded him as the originator of modern evolutionary theory. In one volume of his *Natural History* he tried to trace the history of the earth through seven stages or epochs. Some church thinkers developed the idea into the "day-age theory." Each day of Genesis 1 supposedly corresponded to one of the epochs. The theory was popular during the first part of the nineteenth century, but the "geological-ages theory" eventually replaced it. Science could not make the events described in Genesis fit the evidence from the rocks.

It remained, however, for another French scientist, Lamarck, to formulate one of the first systematic statements of evolution in his *Philosophie Zoologique*, published in 1809. But the scientific community did not generally accept his ideas. Then during 1831-1836 Darwin made his historic voyage around the world. Before considering his work, however, let us go back and note what was happening in the field of geology.

Up until the seventeenth century the people of Europe and America regarded the fossils as *lusus naturae*—"illusions of nature." But in 1669 Niels Stenson (Nicolaus Steno) recognized them as organic remains. Others soon followed his lead, and the idea became generally acceptable. Giovanni Arduinno of Italy made the first attempts to subdivide the geologic record and establish a chronology of earth history. His four categories: (1) primary, the crystalline cores of the mountains; (2) secondary, the limestone and marble flanks of the mountains, generally fossiliferous; (3) tertiary, the unconsolidated sediments of the plains; and (4) quaternary, alluvial material over the surface. From his classification developed the theory that the primary rocks resulted from the cooling of the original molten mass of the earth, the secondary originated during ages of geologic time, and the Flood produced the loose upper sediments.

During the eighteenth century the Flood theory became confused by the teachings of Georges Cuvier (1769-1832), one of the greatest scientists of the late

14

eighteenth and early nineteenth centuries. Famous for his work on comparative anatomy, he developed the theory of successive catastrophes, in which one type of life after another had arisen, only to have some catastrophe overwhelm it. Noah's Flood was the last of the catastrophes. His views, known as classic catastrophism, have no relation to the modern Flood theory of geology now being promoted.

James Hutton, in a paper entitled *Theory of the Earth*, read before the Royal Society of Edinburgh in 1785, introduced geological history in its modern form. He rejected the current Flood theory and went back to the views of the ancient Greeks regarding an old earth. He imagined one cycle after another and concluded that there was "no vestige of a beginning—no prospect of an end." The influence of his discussion turned the attention of geologists to uniformitarianism—uniform action of natural forces.

A young British attorney, Charles Lyell, became interested in Hutton's uniformitarian hypothesis and brought together data from all over the earth to show that all past changes have been of the same nature as those now going on. In 1830 he published his *Principles of Geology*, the first full-scale textbook on geology ever published. Running through twelve editions and used in the colleges of Europe and America for fifty years, it established geological theory along the lines of uniformity rather than catastrophism. By the middle of the nineteenth century, geologists interpreted all their discoveries in terms of uniformitarianism.

But one perplexing problem remained. If the earth was millions of years old, how could this concept harmonize with the generally accepted idea that species had been created and were now the same as at the beginning? Accordingly, when Charles Darwin returned from his voyage on the *Beagle* in 1836 and settled down to ponder the meaning of his observations, he developed a theory of evolution that cleared the way for a full acceptance of geological ages.

Although vigorously opposing Darwin, church leaders seemed strangely at a loss for effective weapons with which to oppose the new ideas. By the middle of the century the growth of geological theory had forced many of them to revamp their view about the days of Creation, and when Darwin introduced his theory, the clergy were no longer sure how to interpret the Book of Genesis.

The chief objections to Darwinism involved the anthropological implications. The clergy objected to the idea of animal ancestry. But their opposition did not hold out long. Aided by the powerful agnosticism of Haeckel and Huxley, modern evolutionary theory won its way rapidly. The Western world gradually came to accept Darwin as one of the great men of his century. His prestige increased, and in 1870 Oxford University gave him an honorary degree. When he died in 1882 he was buried in Westminster Abbey. In 1887 Huxley triumphantly said that theologians had ceased to oppose evolution. Either they denied the reality of Genesis or tried to reconcile it with evolution.

But George McCready Price, a young Seventh-day Adventist high school teacher in New Brunswick, Canada, was studying the problem. In 1902 he published his *Outlines of Modern Science and Modern Chris-*

tianity. Then in 1906 came his *Illogical Geology*, a small, unpretentious pamphlet in which he laid down the main tenets of the Flood theory of geology, which he kept before the world for the next half century. The book made two main points: (1) we have no proof of a succession of life through ages of time, and (2) the uniformitarian hypothesis is "not proved and not provable." Showing the inconsistency of geology as commonly taught, he challenged the scientific world to consider the possibility of the Deluge story of Genesis as an alternative—in fact, the only possible explanation for the rocks of the earth.

Other books and articles flowed from his pen, and in 1923 came his masterpiece, *The New Geology*, the only textbook ever written from the viewpoint of the Flood. Christian colleges used it for many years, and a large number of copies sold, since many people were interested in learning what castastrophic geology had to offer.

A number of other writers followed Price's lead, and for many years books and magazines echoed his ideas on geology. During the years of 1925-45 "Deluge geology" played an important part in the thinking of some conservative and evangelical theologians, even though scientists denounced it bitterly.

In 1920 Price went to Pacific Union College for one year, and I had the privilege of taking his course in geology. For twenty-five years afterward I taught the course, as I remained there in the biology department for thirty-five years. As was inevitable, the new venture into interpretation of a well-established science revealed some problems, and I began an intensive study of them. In 1946 I published my *The New Diluvialism*, setting forth the results of years of research. In it I introduced three new concepts into the Flood theory of geology, now generally accepted by creationists. They are: (1) that the fossils are buried in systematic order and that this order represents the ancient life zones—Ecological Zonation Theory; (2) that a glacial period occurred after the Flood, covering the northern portions of America and Europe; and (3) that terrific tectonic movements had caused great lateral movements, or overthrusts.

Realizing the necessity for deeper study in geological questions, the General Conference of Seventh-day Adventists set up the Geoscience Research Institute in 1957. Not only do its members carry on geological research, but they conduct lectures and institutes and field conferences that give science teachers and others a chance to observe geological formations in the field, thus helping them to interpret geology in terms of the Flood theory.

Walter E. Lammerts, a renowned rose breeder, read *The New Geology* while attending the University of California and became interested in creationism. He felt great concern about the teaching of evolution in the public schools, and in 1963 he and several other creationists met and formed the Creation Research Society. The organization publishes a *Quarterly* in which research papers appear. Its present membership is over six hundred, all of whom must hold a master's degree or higher in natural science and must declare their faith in a literal six-day Creation and a universal Flood. The society is strictly nonsectarian, with members from many different churches.

In 1964 the Bible-Science Association started, with a Lutheran minister, Walter Lang, as its director. Membership is not limited to any church group, but members are expected to subscribe to the same belief as those in the Creation Research Society. Not a research organization, it exists for publicity and promotion. It publishes a monthly *Newsletter*.

One of the most active organizations is the Institute for Creation Research, at San Diego, California. The director is Dr. Henry M. Morris, former president of the Creation Research Society. Associated with it is the Creation-Life Publishers, who distribute books and other printed matter in the field of creationism. The director and others carry on extensive lectures, debates, and other activities promoting creationism.

In 1961 Dr. Morris collaborated with Dr. John C. Whitcomb, Jr., in the publication of *The Genesis Flood*, a book of 518 pages dealing with the Biblical and scientific aspects of the Flood. It has had a wide circulation. *The Genesis Flood* and the author's *Fossils, Flood, and Fire* (1968) are the only books I am aware of that deal (in detail) with the evidences of a worldwide Flood.

The activities of these various groups have led to a great deal of agitation over the teaching of evolution in the public schools. In 1969 the California State Board of Education passed a ruling that texts in biology must contain statements on both creationist and evolutionist views. It created a furor of protest from scientific and educational organizations that raged for several years. Finally the California board amended the ruling to state that the social sciences must present both sides of the evolution-creation question—that a "teacher must be respectful of the commitments of students."

At present a few other states have made moves in the same direction, but most of them have done nothing along this line. However, the various creationist organizations have lobbied for a less biased position. Some local surveys, as for instance at Crescent City and Cupertino, California, have shown that around 90 percent of the parents favor the presentation of both sides of the controversy. Some schools in various states have made creationist literature available.

What the future holds is impossible to predict. But it is evident that many no longer consider creationism as merely a religious dogma. Field research and publication have strengthened its scientific foundation. Creationists, no longer on the defensive, are taking the offensive. One thing is worthy of emphasis—no matter what the religious affiliation—whether Methodist, Lutheran, Baptist, Adventist, or whatever—creationists are working together in the common cause of defending the literal interpretation of the Genesis record of Creation and the Flood.

With this outline of the development of modern evolution and creationism, we will now proceed to study the various problems involved. They fall naturally into two phases—biological and geological. Space permits only scant mention of astronomical questions, as the evidence in that field is almost entirely hypothetical. The greatest problems are the origin of species, of man, and of the fossils. Other minor problems cluster around them, and we will consider them in their relationship to the major aspects.

Chapter 2

New Concepts in Biology

When His Majesty's ship *Beagle* sailed from England in 1831 on a scientific voyage, on board was a young man destined to change the scientific atmosphere of the world. Charles Darwin, twenty-two years old, had tried both medical and theological studies but found them distasteful, although he had graduated from the latter at Cambridge. Desiring to become a successful naturalist, he obtained that position on the *Beagle*.

On the voyage he read the two-volume set of Lyell's *Principles of Geology*, which had just come off the press. The books impressed him and acted as a catalyst for the profound changes that had taken place in his mind.

When the *Beagle* stopped at the Cape Verde Islands, 320 miles off the northwest coast of Africa, he found that while most of the plants were of African types, many species were peculiar to the islands. Science teachers of his day taught that the species of plants and animals had not altered since Creation. Later, as the ship cruised along the coast of Patagonia, he noticed that species showed gradual change from one part of the country to another. But the Galapagos Islands, 650 miles off the coast of Ecuador, particularly impressed him. Here was a whole world of life entirely new to science. When he stepped ashore on the ragged lava rocks hundreds of black iguanas—large black lizards four feet or so long—greeted Darwin. They were unusual because they swam in the ocean and fed on seaweed. He recorded thirteen species of finches, now known as Darwin's Finches. They were all different from their relatives on the mainland and varied from island to island. Some species inhabited only one island.

The islands received their name from the giant tortoise—*galápago*—Spanish for tortoise. They, too, changed from island to island and were adapted to the differing conditions found there.

The greatest variation appeared in the plant life. On Albemarle Island, while 18 species were the same as those growing in other parts of the world, 26 occurred only in the Galápagos Islands, and 22 on that one island. Of the flowering plants he wrote that there were 185 species, 100 confined to the archipelago. He noted 21 species of the sunflower family, 20 existing only there. Also he recognized that all of the life in the islands was of the American type, not like that of the other Pacific islands. Why, he mused, had God created the plants and animals on the islands so much like that of nearby continents, and yet so different. Might not the present species have been the result of changes in the original kinds?

Returning to England, Darwin married his cousin Emma Wedgwood, heiress to the pottery fortune, and settled down to the life of a country gentleman. For fifteen years he labored over the question of the origin of species. He was a good friend of Lyell and became acquainted with other scientists. The Geological Society elected him its secretary.

During this time he read a book by T. R. Malthus which showed that animals increased faster than the food supply. Therefore there would be a competition for existence and only the fittest would survive. Not only would animals struggle against hunger but also against unfavorable climate and other conditions. Then he ran across another clue to what creates new species. On every farm and in many villages lived pigeons. They had come from the native rock pigeon. But how? Simply that when breeders had found interesting variations, they had chosen and preserved them until the original pigeon had become a multitude of different varieties. Why, then, he reasoned, could we not say that nature would select the best stock? The process he called natural selection.

On November 24, 1859, Darwin published the first edition of his book—1,250 copies—which he entitled On the Origin of Species by Natural Selection. It sold out the first day, so great was the public interest in the subject.

When the Origin of Species came from the press the psychological state of the public mind gave it a ready hearing. Many journals ran articles on Darwin's ideas, and many debates occurred. Whethem, in his History of Science, says, "Converging streams of evolutionary thought—cosmological, anatomical, geological, and philosophical, which blocked by the prejudice in favor of the fixity of species, were yet collecting deeper and deeper behind the dam. Darwin's great torrent of evidence in favor of natural selection broke the barrier with irresistible force" (p. 297).

Scientific and industrial advance had undermined religious and social life to such a point that a revolution was bound to come. "Skeptical of the teachings of the Church and impatient of domination by the privileged classes, many could find in the doctrine of natural selection proofs that religion was a failure because the mythological statements of the Bible were contrary to the now easily demonstrated facts of observation" (L. T. More, *The Dogma of Evolution*, p. 9).

In spite of the general trend toward more liberal views regarding Creation, many scientists and theologians opposed Darwin's views. The controversy came to a climax at the meeting of the British Association for the Advancement of Science in June, 1860. It was a victory for Darwin, as his opponents failed to produce scientific evidence against his ideas.

The disciples of Darwin were not slow to grasp the advantages that the changing viewpoints gave them. Defying much that had previously passed for truth, Huxley and others took up the theories of Darwin, translated them into popular language, and presented them to the world as the new gospel for the human family. Later scholars assuaged the wrath of even the orthodox clergy, holding up evolution as the direct means that would usher in the millennium.

Discussion of evolution and creation continued for many years, and by the end of the century nearly everyone had come to accept the idea that the earth was quite old and that the present species of plants and animals had come about through evolution.

In order to understand what a problem Darwin faced, and how it related to the record of Creation as given in Genesis, we must notice some examples of variation. When we have done so, we may be able to derive our own conclusions as to whether he was right or wrong and possibly formulate our interpretation of the data in the light of the Genesis record.

But before we can hope to find a satisfactory answer to the question of where species came from, we need to arrive at a clear concept of what the term "species," as commonly used, actually means. According to the most generally accepted definition, a species is a group of individuals that are alike in form, size, and other characters, in some of which they differ consistently from members of other such groups. They normally and freely interbreed, transmitting their specific characters to their offspring with little or no modification.

While such a definition is true in its general aspects, problems do arise. Some species are constant in their characters, while others are extremely variable. A consideration of members of the dog family will illustrate the difficulties in the way of forming a rigid definition of species.

Linnaeus gave the name *Canis lupus* to all the gray wolves of Europe, most of North America, and a large part of Asia. Those of southwestern North America he labeled *Canis mexicanus*. Later biologists extended the name *mexicanus* to all the wolves of North America, thus separating them from those of Europe and Asia. Eventually scientists divided the American wolves into six species of the genus *Canis*. So we can see that what constitutes a species is largely a matter of opinion of the authorities who classify them.

The problem grows more complicated by the fact that the distinction between wolves, foxes, and jackals is not always clear. Linnaeus at first called the red fox a wolf. The South American foxes are more like wolves than the others. The Arctic foxes are halfway between wolves and foxes. Naturalists at first considered the gray fox as a wolf but later grouped it with the foxes. In India wolves more nearly resemble jackals.

A classic example of the large amount of variation possible, which may result in classification into many species, appears in the Hawaiian group of birds known as honeycreepers. The islands are about 2,500 miles from the mainland, and migration of birds back and forth is rare. No one knows where the first honeycreepers came from, but they were probably emigrants from Central America. The birds have varied so much that biologists have classified them into eighteen genera and forty species. Some are seed-eating birds with heavy bills like those of grosbeaks and parrots. A number have long thin bills for gathering honey from tubular flowers. Still others have a long upper mandible and a short lower one built to enable them to tear away bark and dig out larvae of boring beetles. A few can eat only fruit. But with all this array of species, they are all of one "kind."

Five types of rabbits inhabit the western United States, each adapted to a different environment. The small pygmy rabbit can best live in the scrub of the desert regions. The brush rabbit is next in size, with short legs and ears. Its characteristics fit it for the thickets along streams and roadsides. Next comes the cottontail, which has longer legs, and is adapted to the open woods. In the higher mountains lives the snowshoe hare, much like the cottontail in build. Largest of all is the jackrabbit, whose extremely long legs and ears enable him to survive on the open plains.

How could such differentiation take place? This is the great question, and it will take much study to answer it. But, let us suppose that individuals of a species inhabit a region where climatic changes or other factors might establish a barrier between two portions of the population. Variation in the two groups would be somewhat different, and in time they would become different enough for us to describe them as separate species, even though they might have had a common ancestry.

We see an interesting illustration of changes in a species in the two races of herring gulls that live together in northern Europe without interbreeding. One of them grades off eastward into a subspecies, and it in turn into another, until six subspecies carry the chain around the world. Each one will breed with the one next to it, but the last one in the chain will not breed with the first one of the European gulls. The ability to interbreed seems to decrease gradually, until after circling the polar regions, the differences become so great that breeding is impossible between the two ends of the chain.

Science knows many other such cases of racial circles. They show how barriers against interbreeding may have been built up, thus establishing many of our present species.

An interesting case of actual observation of the origin of a new species occurs in *Spartina stricta*, an indigenous European grass known for about three hundred years. *Spartina alterniflora* is an American species introduced into England that spread somewhat. In 1870 a new form, *Spartina townsendi*, appeared, apparently a hybrid between the European and American species. The new grass was so prolific that it spread rapidly and covered thousands of acres in England and France. Whenever it came into contact with either of its parents it supplanted them. Its superior qualities gave it a selective value that enabled it to withstand the vicissitudes of climate with greater success than could the other species that were already occupying the same territory.

Desert plants, particularly cactus, offer a good example of how plants have become adapted to new conditions. Geological evidence indicates that the present desert regions were once well watered. But as they became more and more arid, many plants found the situation intolerable and died out. The cactus family, able to survive the changing conditions, has thrived and multiplied. Many features fit it for the desert, as for example: (1) a double root system—shallow roots to pick up every bit of rain that falls and a deep system to gather moisture from deep in the sand; (2) a thick, heavy epidermis to protect against drying; (3) a spongy interior capable of absorbing and holding large amounts of water; (4) mucilaginous sap that has less tendency to evaporate than thin sap; (5) chlorophyll in the stem so that the plant can dispense with leaf surface; (6) spines for protection against animals that would relish the succulent stems; and (7) a high degree of tolerance for extremes of heat and cold.

It is quite easy to see that as deserts appeared in various places, several groups of plants—cacti, euphorbias, and others—could endure the developing conditions. They formed the flora of the desert as other less capable ones perished. Here, by the way, is where natural selection plays its part, not in producing new species, but in maintaining something already formed and adjusting it to new conditions. A number of writers mentioned the concept of natural selection before Darwin took it up, but they saw it as something that preserved existing species, not a process that produced new ones.

Another example of adaptation to desert conditions is the spadefoot toad, which only occasionally finds water in which to breed. It (quite commonly), estivates for two or three years without coming out to lay its eggs. When a rain does come, the toads emerge by the millions. When the tadpole has reached one tenth of its normal growth, metamorphosis takes place. The tiny toads are fitted for their peculiar situation by the development of a "spade" on the hind foot, which they use to dig into the ground while awaiting another favorable season.

At the time Darwin proposed his theory of natural selection, it looked good, but he knew little of how variation took place. Before science could obtain a fuller understanding, it needed to know more on what variation is and how it operates.

While Darwin formulated his theory, Gregor Mendel, a priest in the monastery at Brünn, Austria (now Brno, Czechoslovakia) experimented to find out how variation actually operated. Mendel had studied science in Vienna, and afterward had returned to Brünn and taught science at the high school. At the same time he carried on breeding experiments in the monastery garden.

He hybridized different plants and was most successful in his work on the garden pea. After working for several years, he presented the results of his work in a paper read before the Natural History society of Brünn. But his paper, receiving little attention, lay almost forgotten for about thirty-five years until three European scientists simultaneously rediscovered the same principles. In recognition of Mendel's work they called what they had found Mendel's Laws. What are his laws?

If a tall pea (T) crosses with a short pea (t), all the plants of the first generation will be tall. When these cross among themselves, three fourths of them will be tall and one fourth will be short. One of the tall peas will continue to breed true, and the other two will breed in the three-to-one ratio. A diagram will make this clear.

	T	T
t	Tt	Tt
t	Tt	Tt

This relation involves what we call dominance, that is, the tall dominates the short whenever it is present. Even though the seed contains the short factor, it does not show up. The factors for tallness and shortness lie in paired chromosomes in the body cells. When reproductive cells form, the pairs separate, one going to each cell—egg or sperm. Geneticists call it the reduction division because the number of chromosomes is reduced to half as many in the sperm cells as in the regular body cells. The body cells are said to diploid, or double, while the reproductive cells are haploid, or half number. A pea with only tall factors would of course produce eggs or sperms carrying only tallness (T), and a short pea would have eggs or sperms carrying shortness (t). When they unite, it restores the full diploid number, but it is mixed (Tt).

Now let us cross two peas that have mixed characters. As the factors separate, they will be of two kinds, T and t. Then the crossing will look like this:

	T	t
T	TT	Tt
t	Tt	tt

Thus we can see that one fourth are pure tall (TT), one half are mixed tall (Tt), and one quarter are pure short (tt).

Mendel did not know what caused the combination of characteristics. But a few years after he did his work, in 1873, investigators found the chromosomes in the nuclei of the cells. After science rediscovered the laws of genetics, researchers noted that the distribution of the chromosomes in cell division seemed to follow a pattern related to that of the hereditary characters.

Intense research began on heredity, and the science of genetics developed. The most famous geneticist was Thomas Hunt Morgan of the California Institute of Technology, at Pasadena and the Columbia University in New York. He bred thousands of tiny fruit flies in small bottles in the laboratory and studied their heredity. In 1926 he published his *Theory of the Gene*, which opened up an entirely new concept in biology.

Morgan and a host of other research workers found that along the length of the chromosomes are certain loci or spots called *genes*, which control hereditary characters. All they knew about them was that they were apparently some kind of chemical aggregates that, in some unknown manner, caused the development of definite characters such as size, shape, and color of the body or of its parts. A cell might contain as few as two pairs of chromosomes or as many as several hundred in some species. Some of the chromosome maps that Morgan produced from his study of the fruit flies he divided into hundred-unit lengths, with many of them subdivided into decimal parts.

When there are many chromosomes, in the reduction devision each pair separates independently of the others. Thus, if the chromosome of the pair that came from the mother goes to the egg, it has nothing to do with how the other chromosomes will separate.

Sometimes chromosomes break apart and exchange sections—"cross over" geneticists term it. All the genes in one chromosome comprise a unit, and this is known as linkage. There are many details that scientists have still not worked out.

New Concepts in Biology

Sometimes hereditary factors undergo what scientists call mutation. For example, in the fruit fly, researchers have found at least sixteen variations in eye color. They run from pure white to deep red. Nearly all of them result from changes in a single gene.

Breeders have produced hundreds of new varieties of fruit, vegetables, and domestic animals by selecting new variations that show up. The Concord grape appeared suddenly on a vine in Concord, New Hampshire. Growers have propagated it as one of the most desirable of table grapes. The Shirley poppy showed up as a mutation in the fields of England. If a mutation turns up that seems to be desirable, growers breed it until it proves to be true—that is, until they have eliminated any undesirable factors. Eventually they establish a new line of pure characters.

These facts help us understand what apparently has been taking place in nature in the past. If any area inhabited by certain species became separated or broken up by the formation of deserts or by climatic changes or by any other agency that would restrict the distribution of plants or movement of animals, then members of a species on one side of the barrier might develop variations that would make them somewhat different. Biologists refer to such separations as *isolation*.

In South America the wrens are distributed almost continuously, and although they vary widely, they grade into each other imperceptibly. But in some localities isolated patches of wrens occur, with no transitional forms between them and other groups. They have become discrete species. The separate wren populations of the islands off the coast of Scotland have become distinct from one another in a similar manner.

In animals the number of separate species varies according to the freedom with which they roam about. Cedar waxwings range over the whole United States, and one species covers the entire country. Robins travel less widely, and we observe distinctions between the Eastern, Southern, and Western robins.

We should clearly distinguish the isolation factor in the production of new species from natural selection. Where a barrier comes between two populations, variations occurring on the two sides of the barrier may accumulate until they are different enough for us to recognize as separate species, and yet, in this case, the variations may not help the animal adapt any better. One group may not be any better fitted for the environment than the other. In fact, the environment may be the same on both sides. Natural selection, on the other hand, works without a barrier—all the variations occurring in a general population can mingle freely. Here, those variations which are adaptive, that is, which help the individuals possessing them to endure their environmental conditions better, will naturally survive and will thrive at the expense of the less suitably fitted ones,

Physiological barriers are often more effective than geographical and may play an important part in nature. In some cases two forms potentially interfertile may occupy different niches in the same region and may not come together during the mating season. Or they may mature at different periods. Sometimes their fertility period may occur at the same time, but because of differences in psychology, structure, viability, or compatibility of reproductive systems, they may find interbreeding impossible. The physiological barriers thus established would account for the presence of some species of comparatively similar structure in the same territory.

In the Eastern States the small tree *Crataegus*—thorn apple—is extremely variable. Studies on *Amelanchier* (Juneberry), *Crataegus* (hawthorn), and *Rubus* (blackberries) suggest that where environmental influences are uniform, we find only one or two species. But where unusual conditions such as cutting or fire occur, many variants arise, often difficult to classify. I once asked the curator of the Asa Gray Herbarium in Cambridge, Massachusetts, what he did with this problem.

"Well," he replied, "when we find a new form we just give it a new species name and let it go at that."

Here natural selection has nothing to do with the new form. The variation grew right along with the others. Its appearance resulted from a mutation, and its spread was due to what might be called genetic infusion. This means that a genetic change becomes infused into the population of the original type and occupies a certain territory along with those previously there.

An interesting illustration of the distribution of variants is the wild buckwheat, *Eriogonum*. *A California Flora* by Munz and Keck lists seventy-five species in the state, many of which range as far east as the Rockies and northward to Montana. Varying from low mats to tall bushes, they all possess rounded or flattened clusters of white or pinkish flowers, often on long stems.

They are so distinctive that it is easy to recognize a member of the genus at a glance. Seven subspecies of one species has seven subspecies growing in various habitats—coastal bluffs, chaparral, grassland, rocky places in the mountains, and in the forests. All have evidently come from one original kind.

In the deserts of southeastern California lives a spiny bush called saltbush—genus *Atriplex*. Thirty species of it grow in California. Some of them that are soft and succulent are found in the central valley and are commonly known as pigweeds. Others have adapted themselves to the deserts and are tough and spiny. Among the desert species, one reaches up to five feet tall and prefers the drier, cooler parts of the desert. Another one may be twelve feet tall and live along the Colorado River and near the Salton Sea, where they find more moisture. Additional ones are low, rounded shrubs about three feet tall that inhabit saline soils near the dry lakes. It is easy to understand how many of the variants may have arisen from one common ancestry. Natural selection apparently had a part in causing their distribution.

The work of Morgan and his researchers opened up a new vista into what is taking place in nature. But it was Austin H. Clark, of the staff of the National Museum in Washington, D.C., who first came out with a clear distinction between species and the major categories. In 1930 he said, "All the major groups of animals have maintained the same relationship to each other from the very first. The characteristic features of these major groups have undergone no change whatsoever. Crustaceans have always been crustaceans, echinoderms have always been echinoderms, and mollusks have always been mollusks. There is not the slightest evidence which supports any other viewpoint.

"Yet on the other hand *within* each major group there has been constant and continual change" (*Zoogenesis*, p. 114).

The classic experiments of Richard Goldschmidt have a bearing on the problems we are considering. As a young man he became interested in trying to prove the Darwinian theory. While director of the Kaiser Wilhelm Institute für Biologie in Berlin he looked around for some medium with which to work, and he chose the gypsy moth. For twenty-five years he carried on breeding experiments, with several generations of moths produced each year.

During the winter of 1932-33, while I attended the University of California, at Berkeley, he lectured there on his work. During a question and answer period, someone asked him just how evolution worked. His answer was, that as far as gypsy moths were concerned, it simply did not. Whenever he obtained variations that were very far from the common average, they immediately changed back to the norm in a generation or two. He concluded that accumulation of variations leads to diversification strictly *within* the species and are an adaptation to local conditions. They do not result in the development of major groups.

In 1940 Goldschmidt put his ideas into a powerful book that sharply criticized the Darwinian theory of natural selection. While admitting, as he said in his lecture, that many changes take place *within* the genus and species, he denied that natural selection could produce major transformations. He challenged Darwinists to explain such features as hair on mammals, feathers on birds, formation of the gill arches, shells of mollusks, compound eyes, poison apparatus of snakes, and many others. No one has ever successfully answered his book *The Material Basis of Evolution*.

Because of new discoveries, and the issues raised by Clark, Goldschmidt, and others, biologists have been forced to recognize two categories of variation—*macroevolution* and *microevolution*. Macroevolution (great evolution) expresses the idea of the origin of the higher categories, the family, order, class, and phylum. Microevolution expresses the idea of changes *within* the major groups, such as assortment and recombination of genes in each generation, each mutation. All known genetic processes take place in this category. It is unfortunate that scientists use the word *evolution* here, as it is not evolution in the true sense but merely variation. But since it forms the common vocabulary of biologists, we have to use it.

The next morning after his lecture a number of students asked Goldschmidt to go over to the Museum of Vertebrate Zoology, where they had laid out series of different kinds of animals. They pointed to the variation in the series and asked if that did not imply evolution. To the question, Goldschmidt responded that he saw variation all right, but he noted that the rats were still rats, the rabbits were still rabbits, and the foxes were still foxes. He saw no evidence of one kind turning into another.

This is about where the situation has stood for the

38

past quarter century. Creationists have built up their main argument on the basis of the evidence we have presented and have backed their idea with the words of eminent authorities in biology. While creationists have accepted the idea of microevolution, they deny the possibility of macroevolution. Holding to the basic concept that whatever changes do occur are *within* the major kinds and not from one to another, they point out that this concept agrees perfectly with the Genesis declaration that God created plants and animals "after their kinds."

However, creationists have much that they still do not understand. With around two million species of living things on the earth today, how could such a diversity come about in the short time allowed by the Bible chronology that places the Flood only about 4,500 years ago? Certainly we need to know much more about variation before we can explain such a tremendous expansion of species.

The past twenty-five years have not been fruitless. Science has made marvelous discoveries, and great advancement has taken place in the field of genetics and the problem of the origin of species. We shall discuss this further in the next chapter.

Chapter 3

Unlocking the Mystery of Cell Life

So far scientific investigation had shown that variation produces new varieties, species, and possibly new genera. But as yet geneticists had discovered nothing that showed *how* the changes occurred or what was the nature of the genes. Assortment and recombination of already known characters—yes. But how did variation take place? Biologists searched in vain for an answer until in 1953 there came a breakthrough. Studies had shown that the nucleic acid in the chromosomes was the substance that controlled their action in forming protein for the growth of cells.

Then two young scientists at Cambridge University, James D. Watson and F. H. C. Crick, proposed a model for deoxyribonucleic acid (DNA for short). They described it as a double helix, or spiral, something like a ladder, with crossbars between the two sides. The sides of the ladder consist of alternating units of sugar and phosphate, between which—the rungs of the ladder—extend nitrogenous bases. A unit of phosphate, sugar, and a base constitutes a nucleotide. Biochemists have identified four types of bases—adenine (A), guanine (G), thymine (T), and cytosine

Unlocking the Mystery of Cell Life

(C). In the nucleotide a pair of bases, either TA or CG, joins the sugar on one side of the ladder to the phosphate on the other, and these may occur in various combinations and sequences. They are the genetic alphabet that can make an almost endless number of combinations.

Recent reports tell us that the sequence of nucleotides in a certain virus, one of the simplest of all known living structures, consists of 5,374 nucleotides. To write it out in ordinary type, with capital letters, covers a page 7 x 10 inches, with 54 lines. To write the sequence in a bacterial cell would require 2,000 pages, and for a mammalian cell a million pages. This will give an idea of how complex DNA really is. (Clifford Grobstein, "The Recombination—DNA Debate." *Scientific American*, July, 1977, p. 22).

Nucleotide sequences form what geneticists term "codons," or genes. So here, at last, we have begun to discover what genes really are. The sequence in which the codons are arranged determines the order in which amino acids will assemble to form proteins. The sequence is a genetic code.

But how does it happen? In the nucleus a strand of DNA directs the synthesis of a strand of RNA, the "messenger" to carry the code to tiny structures in the outer part of the cell known as *ribosomes*. As the RNA comes to a ribosome, it acts as a template on which the ribosome will build the proteins. Another type of RNA, known as transfer RNA and much shorter than the first, picks up the amino acids from the cell fluid and carries them to the template. Here the ribosome causes them to unite to form the protein the RNA calls

41

for. Scientists have photographed DNA and RNA through an electron microscope, and the pictures confirm the theory of RNA action.

Knowledge of how genes work has important practical consequences. In a significant breakthrough researchers have at last synthesized insulin in the laboratory. After ten months of research, two California laboratories announced they had taken the genes carrying the genetic code for insulin in rats and inserted them into *E. coli* bacterial cells. The genes then activated the *E. coli* to produce protein chains found in insulin. After purifying and isolating them, the scientists combined the two protein chains to create synthetic insulin. Animal insulin now used is about 1 to 2 percent impure and causes severe allergic reactions in some patients, but the new insulin will contain no contaminants.

Such successes will help us to realize to what extent scientists have done research on DNA.

Now what relation does this elaborate mechanism have to the question of the origin of species? It is a well-known fact that slight changes in genes may cause certain diseases. Sickle-cell anemia results from the formation of abnormal red blood cells. Medical science believes that a single defective gene causes it. An extra chromosome in the body cells produces Mongolism, a form of severe mental retardation. Abnormal chromosomes lead to a number of other defects.

It is easy to understand how small changes might occur—mutations, as we call them—from slight modifications of DNA. Many of the criteria that distinguish one species from another are, in the case of plants, differences in size, shape, and color of the plant body, of the leaves, blossoms, and fruit. Plant breeders work on such factors to produce new varieties. The same is true of animal breeding. But if the changes are too great, the new plant or animal may die, or if it lives, it may be deformed or deficient in some way.

Many mutations are known to be neutral—neither harmful nor beneficial. Natural selection would have no basis to separate one of them from another. And yet such mutations might give rise to new species.

The June/July, 1977, issue of *Natural History* contains an article written by Stephen Jay Gould, teacher of biology and geology at Harvard University. Entitled "The Return of Hopeful Monsters," it refers to a theory published by Richard Goldschmidt in his book *The Material Basis of Evolution*. Goldschmidt made a sharp distinction between microevolution and macroevolution. The former he allowed and gave many illustrations, but he did not agree that higher categories of plants and animals arose by gradual and continuous change as Darwin had postulated. He said that many micromutations have appeared in the past, but most of them were disastrous, of no use in the process of evolution. However, once in a while one would appear that would enable an organism to adapt to a new way of life—a "hopeful monster"—and it would give rise to a new category of plant or animal.

Gould argues in favor of Goldschmidt's theory, but he denies that it is contrary to Darwinism. He admits, though, that science has "precious little on the way of intermediate forms; transitions between major groups" in the fossil record is "characteristically abrupt." The way he solves the problem is by assuming that life is "preadapted" so that it can adjust itself to new situations and survive in spite of adverse conditions. It does so by controlling the early stages of development of the embryos, so as to produce something new.

Both Goldschmidt and Gould have missed, as have most evolutionists, the real meaning of preadaptation, however.

An exciting study on the problem appeared in an article entitled "The Mechanisms of Evolution" in the *Scientific American* of September, 1978. Dr. Francisco J. Ayala, professor of genetics at the University of California, at Davis, gave details about the mechanisms of evolution. We will note some of the points that he made:

Most mutations, he said, are harmful, and nature will eliminate them. They cannot hold their own against better adapted forms. But any mutation that is advantageous will spread and gradually replace the original type from which it came. A full-page plate showing twenty-four variations in the color pattern on the wing covers of the Asiatic lady beetle provides an interesting illustration of variation. The patterns range from yellow with a few black spots to red and black with only a few patches of yellow. An insect of each different pattern occupies a specific niche in nature in Siberia, Japan, Korea, and China.

The lady beetle example reminds one of the peculiar distribution of the tree snails found in Hawaii and other Pacific islands. There, one type may occupy one tree; others live in different trees. And often each type appears so different that biologists call them by different species names.

A mutation, Dr. Ayala says, is an "error" in the DNA sequence. Apparently it takes only a slight change in chemical composition to alter the effect of the DNA sequence.

When a favorable change occurs, it may be regarded as a "preadaptation," that is, one that will prove to be adaptable and give the individual a better chance to survive.

Ayala discusses a new method of studying variation, which has an important bearing on the problem of the origin of species. It is electrophoresis, a chemical method too technical for detailed discussion here but which has thrown new light on the problem. Darwin assumed that changes came by mutations, but the new knowledge shows that mutations are a comparatively rare occurrence. Most changes come from reshuffling of genetic material.

The cells store more genetic factors than scientists have generally recognized, and they remain in a state of low frequency until the environment changes. Then they increase under the influence of the new environmental conditions, until they become dominant. Ayala proceeds to tell how the cell maintains the potentialities in reserve, as it were, until changing conditions give them a chance to exert their influence. Whenever any new environmental situation shows up, populations of plants or animals can usually immediately adapt to it.

Leaving now Ayala's discussion, we note some evidences of such change.

New Creationism

The jungles of Burma, Malaya, Vietnam, and the Amazon have animals that look and behave much alike, yet they are not closely related. In Malaya live the long-eared, long-haired gibbons and orangutans, in Africa the chimpanzees, and in South America the spider monkeys. Their appearance, disposition, and habits resemble each other. The Asian lorises have large eyes and hands and feet for grasping, but no tails. They hang upside down from the branches. The pottos replace them in Africa, and the sloths in South America. None of them are in any way related, yet they are almost alike in their habits and appearance.

One of the most interesting cases is that of the water chevrotain, a tiny antelope living in Africa. Dark reddish brown, it has lines of creamy spots running lengthwise along the flanks and white underparts. In South America another animal, the paca, so nearly resembles the water chevrotain that at a little distance one can hardly tell the difference. Yet the paca is a rodent, a close relative of the guinea pig.

The most astounding phenomenon of all occurs among certain rats. In the jungles of the Indonesian island of Celebes dwell large gray rats with white underparts and long tails that are half black and half white. On the grassy plateaus the same species of rats are sandy above and yellow beneath, and only the tips of the tails are white. Another kind of rat has exactly the same coloring as those in Celebes but inhabits the west African jungle. One day a trapper brought in a specimen that was sandy instead of gray. He said he caught it in a grassy area near camp. Then, in South America naturalists noted exactly the same coloring and behavior. Yet the South American animals were opossums.

Here, apparently, nature was ready to fill any niche that appeared as the result of changing environment. She filled the niches, Ivan T. Sanderson of the British Museum reported, "not by all types of animals, for these would not be suitable. Entirely new types of animals make their sudden and inexplicable appearance as if from nowhere. They are not found in the forests that surround the whole cleared area and yet they appear."

In each complex assemblage of plants and animals every species shows a tendency toward continual fluctuating variation, and any variations arising that happen to be better adapted than those already occupying the ground will immediately crowd out their less capable relatives.

Now, if one views all these facts in the light of the Creation record, he can gain a significant insight into the question of where so many species originated. Here is where *preadaptation* comes into its real meaning. Evidently God created living things with a vast storehouse of genetic factors that modern biology is just beginning to recognize. They can undergo almost incredible changes in minor features, thus resulting in new species.

Now that we have begun to crack the genetic code we might relax and think that we have revealed all the secrets of life. But we could not be more wrong. We have only just begun. Lewis Wolpert, writing in the October, 1978, *Scientific American* challenged the molecular biologists with an imposing array of evidence from the experiments he and others have been making. "How does a . . . fertilized egg," he asked, "develop into an intricate system of many different cell types organized in predictable patterns to form a particular kind of adult animal?"

Arms and legs contain the same tissues, but they are arranged differently. Man and chimpanzee have exactly the same cell types, but they differ in the spatial arrangement of the cells. Cat and dog, we might add, show the same phenomenon.

Wolpert's article goes into elaborate technicalities, and we need not attempt to explain them all. But we might add an illustration of our own to emphasize the point.

Two contractors order building supplies—cement, gravel, stone, brick, framing lumber, siding, electric wire, piping, and so on. The suppliers deliver them to the sites. But what determines the kind of house each pile will become? It is the spacing of the materials, the *patterning*, the blueprints, that make the difference. One pile becomes a modest little cottage; the other a mansion. Yet the materials may be the same.

Wolpert says that we are right back where we were before we knew anything about DNA. We have now only learned how the building material is formed, but we do not know where the patterns came from. "Perhaps," he concludes, "we should . . . remember that the study of genetics . . . [is] effective at levels other than the level of DNA, and unless we have the right" perspective, "we do not know what we are trying to explain or where to look for the explanation."

Probably in another ten years, if this book were to

48

be revised, it would read quite different than it does now. Mankind has much yet to learn about the ways of the Creator. The ancient sage declared, "These are but the fringe of his power; and how faint the whisper that we hear of him! [Who could fathom the thunder of his might?]" (Job 26:14, NEB*).

The problem of the major categories remains unsettled, as far as evolutionary theories are concerned.

In the evolution symposium in the *Scientific American* of September, 1978, James W. Valentine wrote an article entitled "The Evolution of Multicellular Plants and Animals." He gave a series of charts depicting the supposed origin of fish, reptiles, mammals, and land plants. Studying the charts, one may notice some interesting facts. For example, he connects the teleostei, bony fishes of the present, with their hypothetical ancestors by only a dotted line, indicating that it is only a conjecture where they came from. The same is true of all modern reptiles. No one can say what line of evolution they followed. It is all the more striking when we study the evolution of the mammals. Paleontologists find nearly all of them only in the Tertiary rocks, the topmost series in the geologic column. Below them occur only a few primitive-appearing forms, apparently related to the reptiles, and it is from them that all the array of mammalian life supposedly arose. But this is all speculation. The author of the article admits that it is not ordinarily possible to determine the characteristics of the mammals from their fossils.

Valentine suggests that in Cambrian "times," at the

---

*From The New English Bible. Copyright, The Delegates of the Oxford University Press and The Syndics of the Cambridge University Press, 1961, 1970.

bottom of the fossil scale, many body plans emerged, but no one can say from where. His idea is similar to what Austin H. Clark proposed in 1930 in his *Zoogenesis*, that all major types have existed from the beginning of life on the earth.

The chart of the mammalian evolution shows all of the major types as independent entities back as far down in the rocks as we have found them. Creationists are confident in declaring that the complexity of the plant and animal kingdoms fails to show proof of descent of one type from another.

But what about the origin of the first living organism? And how did the first DNA come into existence? How much has modern research brought to bear on these intriguing problems?

Richard E. Dickerson, professor of chemistry at the California Institute of Technology, surveyed the problem and found in it many puzzling questions. In his lengthy article, also in the September, 1978, *Scientific American*, he found himself forced to use such expressions as "may be," "perhaps," "possibly," about thirty-five times. He said that the first great problem is which comes first, the nucleic acids or the enzymes that form them. The conclusion is almost mandatory that both must have existed together from the start.

Another question centers around why only a certain twenty amino acids form the components of protein, when so many others might have served with equal effectiveness. It was purely a matter of chance, Dickerson suggests. Nearly all of the amino acids in living cells are levorotatory—that is, they turn a beam of polarized light passing through a solution containing them to the left instead of to the right, as do many others. How could chance, we may ask, have chosen those particular twenty?

One of the most commonly accepted biological laws is that life comes only from life. And the latest research has failed to discredit it.

You may sometimes hear the claim made that since chemists have been able to produce a synthetic amino acid in the laboratory, spontaneous generation may have occurred in nature. But though under laboratory conditions man has formed amino acids, that is a long way from the complex organization of even the simplest bit of living protoplasm. It would be well for everyone to read the article in the *National Geographic* of September, 1976, and to get a new vision of the marvelous complexity of cell life. The odds against spontaneous generation of living matter are so remote as to be practically impossible.

John C. Walton, lecturer in chemistry at the University of St. Andrews, Fife, Scotland, wrote on the subject in *Origins* (Vol. 4, No. 1, 1977). He discussed many aspects of the subject, but we will only mention one. He cited calculations done on the probability of spontaneous generation of various substances. The chance of an amino acid thus forming is 1 in 10 with 80 ciphers after it. And the possibility of a molecule of DNA spontaneously appearing is 1 in 10 with 8,000 ciphers after it. His conclusion is that "the probability of spontaneous synthesis of the smallest cell (or virus) turns out to be unimaginably small." Such calculations, he says, "illustrate the immense amount of organization that went into the production of the first living system. . . .

Purely random chemical combinations cannot account for the origin of life."

"The underlying similarity and unity of biochemical processes imply that life originated only once. The universality of the genetic code . . . point[s] to the same conclusion. . . . The paradox of the origin of the code is removed if the nucleotide sequences were designed and fabricated to couple with the translation machinery and built at the same time. . . .

"Special creation violates none of the basic physical laws. It generates none of the contradictions . . . encountered with the molecular evolution hypothesis. . . .

"The postulate of living structures by external intervention . . . restores order, harmony, and simplification to the date of physics and biology. . . . The value of any given postulate lies in its ability to correlate, simplify and organize the observables. Judged by this standard, special creation suffers from fewer disadvantages than any alternative explanation of the origin of life."

Now let us see if we can picture what things might have been like after the Flood. The real problem for the creationist is how so many new species could have arisen so suddenly.

While we cannot accurately describe the situations prevailing on the earth at the close of the Flood, yet we do have enough data from geology, anthropology, and related sciences to help us gain a general picture. The center of ancient civilization appears to have been the Middle East highlands, until the great valleys of Mesopotamia and Egypt had drained enough to be habitable. Gradually in some areas desert conditions began to appear; and in others, jungle environments. Each would demand different adjustments on the part of plants and animals before they could inhabit the newly developing region. Numerous rapid changes would occur, resulting in new species to replace the original ones. Here is where the reservoir of genetic potentialities we have been discussing would come into play. Preadaptation, as it is known, would enable organisms to take advantage of any new climatic, geological, or geographical situations. Many new species would arise in rapid order, some to become permanent, others to succumb to the pressure from those better adapted to the changing conditions. All this would bring about speciation as we call it, but speciation does not necessarily mean evolution, as we have seen.

Thus we could account for microevolution, but we can assume macroevolution only by extrapolating the evidences for the development of species to explain the higher categories, and we have as yet nothing but speculation in this line.

Some evolutionists, while fully committed to the theory of origin of species by natural selection, admit that it does not have all the answers. The following appears in a paper by Paul Ehrlich and L. C. Birch entitled "Evolutionary History and Population Biology" (*Nature*, Vol. 214, 1967).

"Our theory has become one which cannot be refuted by any possible observations. . . . No one can think of ways to test it. Ideas, either without basis or based on a few laboratory experiments carried out in extremely simplified systems have attained currency far beyond their validity. They have become part of an evolutionary dogma accepted by most of us as part of our training."

Chapter 4

The Great Catastrophe

Whenever one talks to an evolutionist about the evidences of Creation, no matter how convincing an argument he may offer he always gets the same question: But what about the geological record?

The world in general believes that the rocks are millions of years old and that life must have developed progressively throughout all time. Even some creationists hold that the geological record unquestionably proves long ages.

In the seventeenth century when men began to be interested in the rocks, they saw in them evidences of Flood action. A number of writers attempted to explain the action of the Flood. Their attempts became known as the old diluvianism, or Flood theory, from the Latin *diluvium*, "a flood." But near the end of the eighteenth century a different attitude developed, largely due to the work of James Hutton. When in 1785 he presented his paper, "A Theory of the Earth," to the Royal Society of Edinburgh, he revived the ancient Greek theory that all action in the past had gone on uniformly. Geology calls the view *uniformitarianism*.

About the same time a British land surveyor,

William Smith, noticed that certain fossils always occurred in the same rock formations. He collected a large number, and eventually donated them to the British Museum. Also he made the first geological map of England, in which he outlined the outcroppings of the different layers. Thus he laid the foundation for the modern system of classification of the rocks by means of the fossils.

At that time the most important rocks in the British Isles were the coal beds then known as the Coal Measures, or Carboniferous rocks. Below them, but above the granite foundation, stretched a group of previously unclassified rocks. In 1822 Adam Sedgwick, professor of geology at Cambridge University, began to study them in Wales and western England. About the same time Sir Roderick Murchison, head of the British Geological Survey, conducted similar studies. After some controversy over details, British geologists finally set up a classification that made four divisions of the rocks below the Carboniferous. Each division had its own typical assemblage of fossils. (American geologists eventually subdivided the Carboniferous in the United states into the Mississipian and Pennsylvanian).

Further studies arranged the rocks above the Carboniferous. The table of "The Geological Time Scale" shows the arrangement of the periods (systems, creationists call them) as the science of geology now recognizes them. Note the characteristic life of each.

The relation between this method of classification and the theory of evolution should be made clear. According to the theory that the fossils represent

The Great Catastrophe

THE GEOLOGICAL TIME SCALE
(As commonly taught)

Eras	Periods	Characteristic Life
CENOZOIC	QUATERNARY RECENT PLEISTOCENE	MODERN LIFE GLACIAL TYPES
"Recent Life"	TERTIARY PLIOCENE MIOCENE OLIGOCENE EOCENE	BIRDS MAMMALS HARDWOOD FORESTS FLOWERING PLANTS
	PALEOCENE	SIMPLE MAMMALS
MESOZOIC "Middle Life"	CRETACEOUS JURASSIC TRIASSIC	REPTILES, INSECTS CONIFEROUS FORESTS CYCADS
PALEOZOIC	PERMIAN PENNSYLVANIAN	REPTILES, AMPHIBIANS, SHARKS FERNS, SPORE TREES
	MISSISSIPPIAN DEVONIAN	FISHES, MOLLUSKS BRACHIOPODS, SEED FERNS
"Ancient Life"	SILURIAN ORDOVICIAN CAMBRIAN	MARINE INVERTEBRATES SEAWEEDS TRILOBITES
ARCHAEOZOIC "First Life"	ALGONKIAN ARCHAEAN	TRACES of ALGAE and SIMPLE ANIMALS NO FOSSILS

remnants of the succession of life through the ages, we should be able, by simply looking at the layers of rock and their contained fossils, to tell the order in which they had been laid down. Of course that would give us only the relative time sequence. We would need to use some other method to find the approximates ages.

One technique suggested in the past, which has proved to be practically valueless, is to estimate how long it would take to lay down an inch of sediment and then divide the thickness of the sediments by that figure. Another method was to attempt to determine the time it would take for the oceans to accumulate their salt. The difficulty in both methods is no one can say that the action has been uniform.

In recent years geology has developed radiometric techniques that are assumed to be much more accurate. Certain elements disintegrate and throw off radioactive elements. Uranium may have an atomic weight of 235 or 238, the relative weight of the nuclei. Hydrogen is the lightest of the elements, with a weight of 1. Other elements have different weights, up to uranium, which is the highest.

Uranium-238 is radioactive and disintegrates through a series of 14 intermediate products until it finally becomes lead-206. The change goes on constantly at such a rate that in 4,500,000,000 years it will lose half its substance. This is known as the half-life. By calculating the proportion of uranium-238 to lead-206 in a sample of rock, one can theoretically estimate how long the process has been going on since the uranium-bearing rock cooled from a molten condition.

When a rock is molten, the lead in it volatilizes—

that is, turns to vapor—and escapes. On cooling, the amount of lead present will be zero. Thus the "time clock" starts over whenever the rock melts. Thus geologists assume that we can obtain the time since the rock cooled.

They take for granted that the earth was once molten, but the creationist cannot accept this assumption. If God created the earth by divine command, no one knows in what condition it was originally. But it is perfectly possible that a mixture of uranium and distintegration products may have come into existence at the time of Creation. In the terrific demonstration of power evident in the act of Creation, it is reasonable that a certain amount of change might have occurred when God produced the elements of higher atomic weights. If such transformations took place in as short a time as the amount of power might suggest, they would have appeared to have required great ages for their production.

Competent scientists have stated that the reason we cannot alter the rate of atomic disintegration in the laboratory is that the forces binding the atoms together are so great we cannot approach them by any natural means. But in atomic explosions they break down instantly, helping us to realize what profound changes might have occurred during Creation. Also, could it not have been possible for some great changes to have taken place during the upheaval of the Flood? Such questions we cannot answer, but they do suggest possible sources for the distintegration products of radioactive substances on some other basis than millions of years of radioactivity.

Recent reports tell of many discrepancies in the results of tests on the age of rocks. We will note a few of them.

In New Zealand, trees dated 225 years old by the carbon-14 method (we will discuss that method later) lay under volcanic material that dated from 145,000 to 465,000 years. In 1801 the volcano Hualalali erupted in Hawaii, and tests on the lava indicated an age of over a million years. Datings from a single flow in the Pacific Northwest gave variations of several hundred million years.

Next we will briefly discuss the carbon-14 method. Nitrogen has an atomic weight of 14, carbon of 12. Cosmic rays, powerful energy units entering the atmosphere from outer space, collide with some of the nitrogen atoms, causing such alterations in their structure that they turn into carbon. But the atomic weight has not changed, so now we have atoms of carbon with a weight of 14—carbon-14.

Carbon-14 is unstable and disintegrates slowly. At present the rate of formation and of disintegration is supposed to be balanced, although some people question as to whether this is true or not. Most of the carbon-14 units with atmospheric oxygen to produce carbon-14 dioxide or radioactive carbon ($C^{14}O_2$), and along with ordinary $C^{12}O_2$, plants build it into their tissues. From them it passes on into animals. Thus we find in every living thing a mixture of the two kinds of carbon. But when an organism dies, and the exchange of carbon ceases, the disintegration of the carbon-14 causes it to lose its balance with carbon-12. Knowing the time it would take for carbon-14 to reduce to its half amount—a little over 5,500 years—the chemist can, by finding the ratio between the two carbons, determine how long it has been since the tissues died.

In the past, scientists have observed that C^{14} became erratic beyond about 3,500 to 4,000 years ago. But in *Science* of April 7, 1978, P. M. Grootes, in an article entitled "Carbon-14 Time Scale Extended," reports that new methods now being used extend the dating by means of carbon-14 to 75,000 years. It is, he says, apparently precise and accurate. The method is too technical for discussion here.

The creationist can, if Grootes's report holds good, no longer argue for the inadequacy of the carbon-14 method on the basis of inaccuracy. He will have to take a position something like this: If evolution is true, then we must accept the carbon-14 dates. But if not, if the short chronology is correct, then we must find some other explanation.

The Beresovka mammoth found in the Lena River Delta of Siberia has been carbon-14 dated at 26,000 years, while peat only eighteen inches above gave a date of 5,610 years. Normal growth of that much peat would require only about 2,000 years. Muscle tissue from the scalp of a musk-ox showed an age of 24,000 years, while hair from the hind limb registered only 7,200 years. Ivory from a mammoth skeleton at Rawlins, Wyoming, indicated an age of 11,550 years, while wood in the same gravel dated 5,000 years. The preceding examples represent only a few of the results that are so variable they throw serious question on the method's validity.

Did the atmosphere before the Flood have any

carbon-14? We have no way of knowing. Coal shows none of it as a rule, but geologists assume it is so old that the carbon-14 would all have disintegrated. On the other hand, if the Flood theory with a short chronology is true, the coal should have some if it really did exist. And so the creationist assumes that carbon-14 formed after the Flood, or flood action entirely destroyed it.

unbelievable

After the Flood it would take many years to build up its concentration to balance formation and decay. On that basis we would expect examinations of material buried soon after the Flood to show a low concentration and thus the objects would appear to be much older than they really are. Tests on charcoal and bones found in caves in Morocco and on the south shore of the Caspian Sea produce dates from 30,000 to 40,000 years. Those who accept the Flood as valid must recognize that men inhabited the caves after the Flood, not before. According to our theory, they are not true dates, but need adjusting to correlate with the real ages of the materials. Because of the difficulties in carbon-14 dating, many physicists now use the expression "carbon-14 years" and refuse to say how they relate to the actual chronology.

Another widely publicized method of dating is that of the bristlecone pines of California. At the 10,000- to 12,000-feet elevation exist several groves of apparently ancient trees. They are twisted and gnarled into fantastic shapes, and many of them have little bark on them. Tree-ring counts have placed the age of some of them at 4,600 years. Creationists do not worry much about that, but when recent reports claimed to date some of them at 8,000 years, it raised a question and led to several studies on the problem.

Harold S. Gladwin, of the Santa Barbara Botanical Garden, published an article in the June, 1978, *Creation Research Society Quarterly*, in which he sharply criticizes the conclusions that some have reached by this method.

All trees are not equally valuable in tree-ring dating, he found. Junipers often grow multiple rings a year. Among the pines, the bristlecone pine is the least dependable because so much of it is dead. Sometimes only a few inches of the circumference of the trunk will have any live wood, which makes it practically impossible to obtain continuous cores. It requires much speculation to try to match various sections of live wood.

Gladwin says that cores from different parts of the country fail to show similarity when charted. Also disagreement exists between the ring counts and carbon-14 tests.

In the June, 1976, issue of *Creation Research Society Quarterly*, H. C. Sorenson examined the methods used on the bristlecones. In some cases as many as 30 percent of the counts are extra rings, and in other cases 10 percent are missing. Cross matching is subjective and depends on the ability of the investigator. The rings, he states, are not sufficiently clear to make sure that the counts are correct. Furthermore, the entire chronology has come out of only one laboratory and has not been checked by the findings of other workers.

But what about the record from the stratified rocks? How can we interpret it in terms of the Flood theory of geology? Perhaps the best way to answer that would be to visit some region where we can see the rocks clearly exposed and discover what we can learn from them. Probably nowhere else could we find a better area than in the Colorado Plateau and the surrounding area, sometimes known as the intermountain region. Let us begin at the Grand Canyon in northern Arizona and go northward through Utah, portions of Colorado, Wyoming, Montana, and into other nearby locations.

In central Utah the Colorado River, which originates in Colorado, meets the Green River from Wyoming, and a bit farther down, the San Juan in Arizona. The water from these and many smaller streams contributes to the great bulk of the Colorado as it flows through the Grand Canyon. Today the river is laden with silt, and it must have had a powerful cutting action on the rocks over which it flows. Geologists tell us that it took about 5,000,000 years to carve out the canyon. But is it necessary to have so much time? Evidence indicates that in the past the climate of the region was much more humid than at present, indicating that a much greater volume of water flowed down the river than at present. Cutting would have been much faster than now.

Looking down into the canyon, we can see thousands of feet of sedimentary rock classified as Paleozoic. The sediments contain marine life in the bottom layers, with some plant life higher up. Obviously the area once contained a sea, and when the Flood overwhelmed the earth, the mud washed into the sea, buried its creatures, and formed the marine beds. Higher up on the canyon walls, and especially on the north rim, lie beds of Permian rocks. The Pennsylvanian layers seem to be missing from a large part of the area, but the Permian is much like it. The fossils represent many kinds of plant life and some land animals, such as amphibians and others, that could live around the shores of the sea.

North of the canyon, stretching far into Utah, are the brilliant "red beds," so called because of the large amount of red sandstone.

At another spot, near the campground where the Green River passes through a gorge in Split Mountain, is a display of 16,000 feet of rocks turned up on edge, revealing nearly all of the strata that exist in central Utah. In the region south of the gorge we know them only from well logs, but here they are spread out before our eyes.

The rocks of this region cover about 200,000 square miles. It is difficult to postulate conditions that would deposit thousands of feet of sandstone, shale, and often masses of pebbles, over such a vast area. No river on earth is doing such a thing today. The Amazon has a mouth about a hundred miles wide and brings down water from as much as 3,000 miles away, but what is it depositing? Only fine mud. We observe no sandstone or coarse gravel of any kind.

One of the most remarkable formations in the Colorado Plateau is the Shinarump formation. A greenish layer, running from a few inches up to a hundred feet thick in places, it extends for a hundred or more miles. The layers are generally not more than ten feet thick. How could ordinary streams of water spread out such material so far and wide?

The mystery deepens when we realize that the conglomeration consists largely of rounded pebbles, usually not more than an inch or two in diameter, embedded in a clay matrix. Think of the great "cement mixer" that must have been at work grinding up rocks and making all the pebbles to cover such a vast area.

Where did this material all come from? The mountains in the area arose after the deposits were made, so they did not contribute anything but superficial material later. Geologists recognize no source that they can clearly point to, except for indications that much of it came from an unknown continent to the west and southwest.

Another remarkable feature is that in all the vast region, where today we find mile after mile of cliffs exposed, we observe no evidence of great canyons having formed in past ages. If the deposits had accumulated during a period of 70,000,000 years, as generally supposed, why do we not see large canyons cut into some of the layers? On the contrary, the land appeared to have been low, with meandering streams rushing over it and bringing incredible amounts of sediment. Geologists estimate that the water deposited a million cubic miles of sandstone. Utah is said to be the greatest sand pile in the world.

Travelers in the region may observe an interesting phenomenon. Driving eastward along the Colorado River, they begin to climb into the higher parts of the Rocky Mountain region. The flat layers of rock seen all over Utah and western Colorado now begin to tilt upward, with the higher ends of the tilt toward the east. Eventually a granite core, which forms the Rocky Mountains, rises thousands of feet. It is this uplift that has pushed the layers up on edge.

At the eastern edge of the mountains we encounter the same sedimentary rocks turned up on edge against the eastern flank of the granite core. Just west of Boulder, Colorado, great sandstone cliffs known as The Flatirons stand out sharply against the sky.

The flat sandstones and other rocks that now spread out in layers over the Colorado Plateau and on the plains were once continuous over the entire region. Then when the Rocky Mountain granites thrust up in a semimolten state, they shoved the sediments up for thousands of feet. While that happened, and probably for a long time afterward, tremendous amounts of sand and clay washed to the east over the surface of the plains and to the west into basins between the mountains.

The deposits, classified as Tertiary, are much looser than the beds below them. They have eroded into badlands in many places—in the Uinta Basin, in New Mexico, South Dakota, and other places.

After the uplift of the Rocky Mountain region and the production of the Tertiary deposits, a period of violent volcanic activity followed in some parts of the West. Flows of lava and deposits of volcanic ash, which has formed different kinds of comparatively soft rocks, now cover much of Idaho, parts of eastern Oregon and Washington, and some of western Wyoming.

As we have followed the rocks from the bottom of the Grand Canyon to the top of some of the highest mountains, the question of the validity of the rock sequences naturally arises. Are the rocks over this whole area, in fact over the whole of North America,

Europe, and most of the world, really in some kind of regular sequence? The geologists say they are and give them names and dates involving millions of years. Is it possible to explain all the strata, recognize them as having definite order, and still not be obliged to accept the theory of long ages of geological time?

What do we mean by the sequence of the fossils? We must make one point clear—it is not a progression from simple animals like amoebas up to higher animals and man. It is rather a definite sequence of assemblages of many kinds of animals in different levels. Even in the lower layers we meet highly specialized forms.

The typical fossils of any geological formation are nothing more or less than natural communities of living things that once associated together in the same manner we find them today. The communities distributed themselves according to the environmental conditions—salinity of water, degree of the water's quiet or turbulence, amount of light available, and so on. Burial of ancient communities, or life zones, would produce fossil assemblages, each one representing a natural habitat group.

This interpretation of the orderly arrangement of the fossils as an alternative to the "geological-ages theory" that I first presented in my *New Diluvialism* in 1946 under the term "Ecological Zonation Theory." A brief analysis of this viewpoint follows. It is based on a comparison between the fossil zones and the life zones found on earth today.

Living things on the earth today are arranged in what scientists call life zones, communities, or associations. Each is a network of plants and animals adapted to the environment. For instance, in the middle zone of the Sierra Nevada mountains of California is the pine belt, dominated by the western yellow pine. In the Rockies, in the same ecological zone, is the same yellow pine, but with other plants different from those in the Sierra. The yellow pine is dominant in each locality, and biologists use it as an indicator. It is similar to what paleontologists term "index fossils" for the fossil zones.

The waters of the earth show zoning as do the lands. Marine zones occur over the whole world. Modern texts on zoogeography present a wealth of evidence for the orderly arrangement of animals and plants in the seas as well as on land. Nearly all marine zones are as exact as those on land.

If one were to postulate a direct creation by an omniscient Creator, he would find certain assumptions almost unavoidable, as for example:

1. The earth's surface would be diversified by mountains, plains, lakes, seas, and streams at different levels.
2. The various features would provide homes for many different types of plants and animals.
3. The plants and animals would be grouped in communities according to their adaptation to the environment.
4. If a major catastrophe overwhelmed such a world, it would form a series of deposits in which the fossil zones would roughly approximate the original arrangement of the ecological zones.

Of course we must recognize that there would be a

degree of irregularity, inasmuch as the violence of the Flood would do some mixing, and currents would carry some organisms a distance from the site where they lived. But the fact that we observe any order or system at all in the fossils gives proof that there must have been such in the ancient world. What geology texts have designated as "ages" of time may be interpreted as "stages" of Flood action, of the burial of ancient landscapes.

My *Fossils, Flood, and Fire* (1968) devotes a whole chapter to this subject.

Lanny H. Fisk, assistant professor of paleobiology at Walla Walla College, in a graduate paper, "An Ecological Trend in Trilobites" (Loma Linda University), reports on a test case for the theory of ecological zonation. He made a special study of the distribution of the fossil trilobites. There were three types—benthonic, that live in the mud; nektonic, that are able to swim; and planktonic, that are free floating. They were stratigraphically distributed in the order given.

Fisk cites a report by La Rocque and Marpel (1955) in their book on *Ohio Fossils*. The ones in the Ordovician strata were smooth, with little ornamentation. In higher strata the ornamentation increased, and those in the Pennsylvanian rocks had extensive ornamentation with spines that enabled them to float.

The most comprehensive study yet made along this line appeared in the September, 1978, *Creation Research Society Quarterly*. John Woodmorappe made a detailed study of the distribution of fossil Cephalopods. They are marine Mollusca, comprising 10,000 species, few of which exist today. The best-known illustration of the group is the chambered nautilus, a coiled animal resembling a squid in structure, but with the addition of a shell.

The animals are, the author stated, the most complex, the most advanced, and the most studied of all the invertebrates. Scientists have generally considered them as providing the "stiffest challenge to Diluviology." The paper attempted to give an ecological explanation for the order in which the Flood deposited them. The article is technical, and we shall cite only a few points to show its significant conclusions.

One of the greatest problems in the fossil record of Cephalopods, Woodmorappe pointed out, is the imperfection of the successional order. It is so frustrating to the evolutionist that he finds it impossible to map out any path for evolution owing to the infinity of missing links. The author then proceeds, by several pages of technical discussion, to show how the Cephalopods illustrate Creation better than they do evolution. Much of the attempted "correlation" of Cephalopod zones in the world, on an evolutionary basis, he stresses, is purely arbitrary.

Evidences for cataclysmic burial commonly show up among the creatures. The nature of the specimens themselves, their arrangement in the fossil beds, make a uniformitarian explanation incredible. Once we accept that such an interpretation is invalid we must view all fossil successions as primarily ecological. It is easy to see how God designed the different types of Cephalopods for a specific ecological habitat. The same factors that govern marine ecology today appear in the fossil sequence. In conclusion he states that the marine

71

invertebrates "provide an amazing amount of evidence" for the Creation-Flood model.

Woodmorappe suggests how Flood activity could have made the Cephalopod fossils seem to succeed each other. Not all diluvialists will agree with every detail, but that is a matter of personal opinion as to details of Flood action. It in no way detracts from the validity of his general conclusions.

I cite such facts as evidence that there was zonal distribution of animals in the ancient seas and that they were buried in the order of their occurrence.

Some creationists do not fully agree with the zonation theory, but most of the objections come from those whose views of the rocks differ from the majority of conservative creationists. Anyone who believes that the earth is much older than six thousand years and that it went through a series of catastrophes in the "ages" preceding Creation Week would, naturally, not be able to adjust ecological zonation to his way of thinking. And anyone who still holds to the idea that the fossils have no sequence will see no significance in it.

Chapter 5

Fossil Zones

Now that we have considered some of the evidence for an overwhelming flood and presented the theory of ecological zonation, it might be well to begin at the bottom of the rock series and trace the fossils up through the "geological column"—through the different systems. While doing so we will note some of the terrific forces that have been at work during the burial of the fossils.

The older diluvialism, or Flood theory, current in the eighteenth and nineteenth centuries, disappeared before the Hutton-Lyell uniformitarian theory. Then when George McCready Price introduced the modern Flood theory of geology about 1900, there arose what we call the "new diluvialism," or the interpretation of geology in terms of the Flood in light of recent discoveries. As the twentieth century has progressed, more and more details have come to light, and it has become possible to construct a fairly reasonable picture of the major processes going on during that great catastrophe, although we lack much detail. And so let us begin with a general view of the earth as a whole and trace the rocks upward and study their formation.

The interior of the earth possesses an extremely dense core, probably of iron and nickel, over which lies a mantle of heavy rocks, and on that a thin crust. The crust is about 5 to 20 miles thick, the mantle and the core approximately 1,400 to 2,000 miles each. Sediments of shale, sandstone, and limestone comprise the crust, with underlying crystalline rocks, largely granitic in nature. The mantle is of glassy, probably semimolten, materials.

In our study of the Flood we are not concerned with anything but the crust, so we shall start with the crystalline rocks lying below the sediments—the Precambrian. They are located mostly in what geologists call shields, such as the Canadian, the Baltic, and the Angara in northeast Asia. The rocks of the Canadian shield are best for our study. Lying in the northeastern part of North America, they consist of fine crystalline material. Except some small ones such as worms, bacteria, and such, they lack fossils. Often they are banded with light and dark layers, sometimes with pink and gray, making a beautiful appearance. Often they are twisted and distorted.

Diluvialists have generally considered Precambrian rocks as having been in position before the Flood, but recent studies have made some revision necessary. The banded section that we have been describing is the upper, or Algonkian section. Below it is the Archaean, which consists of crystalline rocks such as granite, basalt, and such. Paleontologists have found no fossils there.

The presence of even the simplest fossils in the Algonkian portion would lead us to believe that it represents the muddy bottoms of the antediluvian seas, suitable habitats for only simple organisms. The boundary between them and the Cambrian is not always easy to define, although the latter is generally rich in fossils.

Geologists have observed reefs of algae tens of feet thick in the Precambrian and stony, cuplike sponges associated with algal reefs in the Cambrian. Other animals also appear. Red algae and corals appear in the Ordovician. It seems a natural situation for the occurrence of reefs in the antediluvian waters. In many places in the Canadian shield, extensive intrusions of granite have come up through cracks in the layers, doubtless due to the violence of the Flood.

The lower fossiliferous rocks are the Paleozoic—ancient life. The first three—Cambrian, Ordovician, and Silurian—are so much alike that we may consider them together. They present to the evolutionists a perplexing problem, for how could such a vast assemblage of complex forms have come into existence without ancestors?

One of the best exposures of Cambrian fauna is the Burgess shale near Field, British Columbia. It contains remains of many soft-bodied animals resembling flowers in a press and perfectly preserved. Paleontologists have described as many as 130 species from a bed only a few feet thick. In all North America the Cambrian strata contain more than twelve hundred kinds of animals. About 60 percent are trilobites. Related to the crabs, they resembled pill bugs. Varying in size from an inch up to two feet long, they grubbed along the bottom of the seas for food. None are alive today. Next in importance were the brachiopods. They looked like clams, but attached themselves to the sea bottom by stalks.

Cambrian is well exposed in North America, sometimes at the surface as in the mountains of the West, sometimes in deep sediments as on the plains. Typical deposits begin with massive sandstone or quartzite, the bottom of which has several feet of conglomerate or breccia. Conglomerate contains rounded pebbles of various sizes, while breccia consists of broken fragments that have not been rolled around enough to break off the sharp edges.

The massive sandstones, quartzites, and their coarse constituents grade upward into shales and limestones.

The question arises, Why do we see evidence of a worldwide distribution of these coarse sediments at the bottom? Where did the clastics (rocks made up of fragments of other rocks) come from? It would seem that they must have come from the wash-off at the initial stages of the Flood action. They, being composed of coarse fragments, would have settled first, and later, the finer sediments.

Ordovician and Silurian strata have much the same life-forms as the Cambrian, with an abundance of corals, crinoids, and clams. Crinoids, related to starfish, are borne on the tops of long stalks and have acquired the name sea lilies. Some Silurian limestone consists almost entirely of crinoids.

Devonian rocks also contained vast amounts of fish skeletons. The fish are called armored fish because of a heavy plate covering the front part of the body. A few simple plants appear in the Devonian.

Fossil Zones

Most of the animals found in the lower Paleozoic rocks continue up into the Permian. The rocks are similar in nature throughout, and only by their fossil assemblages can geologists distinguish between them. The exact classification of these systems is difficult, as certain areas lack some of the members. But the fact that certain groups of animals occur more frequently in one zone than in another strongly suggests local habitats, such as we find in the oceans today.

The Ordovician rocks of the Appalachian region contain large amounts of black shales. Geologists do not understand their origin well, but many believe them to have formed from ancient soils. Or they may have developed in local depressions such as we see now in the Baltic region, where the bottom contains fine muddy sediments.

The whole Appalachian region was once a great waterway or system of waterways, with islands and local areas of land that allowed trees to grow along the water. So, when we come to the Pennsylvanian strata, we find a marvelous array of plant life. Quite different from anything existing today, it contained huge ferns and other spore-bearing trees. The most striking were the "scale trees," so called because of the scalelike scars left by the dropping of the leaves. They grew four to six feet in diameter and over a hundred feet tall.

Lepidodendron was a scale tree that branched repeatedly and bore a bunch of slender leaves resembling huge pine needles. Spore cases looking like cones grew on the ends of the branches. Paleontologists report about a hundred species.

Giant scouring rushes grew thickly in portions of

the lowlands. Some of them were a foot in diameter and thirty feet high. When included in the coal, they form clinkers because of the large amount of incombustible silicon they contain.

In the Pennsylvanian rocks, land animals begin to appear, including about seventy-five kinds of amphibians, some of them ten or more feet long. Insects were common. Cockroaches were up to four inches long and had a wingspread of nearly two feet. Starfish are the most common fossils in Pennsylvanian rocks.

One peculiar feature of these rocks is the occurrence of cyclothems, where one finds many kinds of rocks, particularly limestone and sandstone, alternating as much as ten times in a thousand feet of sediment. The members vary in thickness. In the Midwest they average less than fifty feet. West Virginia has ninety cyclothems showing shallow shifting and other evidences of rapid changes. They contain many features that indicate formation by the Flood.

Of worldwide occurrence, some cyclothems in the coal beds extend for four hundred miles. The American and European varieties are similar. They appear to have been deposited in shallow seas rather than in deep water, indicating just what one would expect of a great flood of waters rushing over lowlands. In addition they give evidence of cataclysmic burial, in a rapid alternation of shale, the rock pebbles interstratified with the fine material. The presence of polystrata trees, with trunks extending up through many layers, is significant. Such a situation would be impossible unless the sediment surrounding them was deposited rapidly.

Fossil Zones

Every alternate layer, no matter how small, represents a separate movement of water.

Geology texts place much emphasis on what they call great deltas in the Pennsylvanian rocks. It is apparent from the nature of the rocks in the Appalachian region that a large landmass once lay off to the east. Streams rushing down from the highlands deposited a succession of sand, shale, and other materials, reaching nearly the whole length of the region. Vigorous currents took up some of it and carried the finer materials far out over the central area. In fact delta action extended as far west as Colorado and New Mexico.

The Pennsylvanian coal beds have created much discussion about the method of their formation. Popular theories explain them as having developed in bogs over a period of 6,000,000 years. But the theory faces great difficulties. It is not necessary to have bogs for the growth of giant ferns and other plants such as show up in the coal. In Hawaii today tree ferns occur luxuriantly without swampy land.

The bog theory would require that the whole area, of several hundred square miles, be delicately balanced and rise and sink over and over to alternate plant growth with burial in mud and sand. The process would have to go on from fifty to one hundred times and continue for millions of years. Such a condition is hard to imagine.

If such alternations have gone on naturally, every time the land sank or rose it should have formed a series of sea beaches. But we observe no evidence of any.

A striking feature of coal beds is the presence of

boulders. They have turned up all over the world. Forty boulders collected in West Virginia had an average weight of twelve pounds, and one of them weighed 161 pounds. Many of them were of igneous (volcanic) rock, unlike any known in the area. It implies that the deposits were made by washing or wave action, not by natural bog formation.

Marine fossils are common in the coal beds. Since we have no indication that coal plants were adapted to marine conditions, their presence suggests that the fossils must have washed in from a distance.

Heavy clay often underlies coal beds, which some geologists have interpreted as a soil in which the plants grew. But the underclay does not resemble modern soils. It shows bedding features that seem to indicate washing. Many coal beds rest on granite or on other rock, with no sign of underclay.

Above the Pennsylvanian and the Permian lie another great series of rocks, the Mesozoic, made up of three systems—Triassic, Jurassic, and Cretaceous. They are the "red beds" that we spoke about in the previous chapter. Jurassic rocks are famous for their dinosaur remains. The Morrison formation, extending over a large expanse of the Rocky Mountain region, contains the greater number of those discovered. Spread out over more than 100,000 square miles and only 400 to 500 feet thick, it gives evidence of violent washing. It is a terrestrial formation, with no marine fossils.

Near Vernal, Utah, is the Dinosaur National Monument. Bones pack a sandstone bed 150 feet long and 50 feet high. Against the cliff the government has erected a building, where visitors may stand on the balcony and view the exposed bones. The bones are badly scattered about, another indication of violence.

Some of the reptiles were tremendous. *Diplodocus* was around 85 feet long; *Brontosaurus*, about 65 feet long. Recently a report tells of discovery of a dinosaur over 100 feet long. There were many kinds, such as the *Pterodactyls*, or flying reptiles, and *Ichthyosaurs*, or fishlike reptiles. In fact, the reptiles had as many diverse forms as all the land mammals together.

The sudden disappearance of these great beasts has greatly puzzled paleontologists. None of them appear in the rocks above the Mesozoic. What happened to them? The area they inhabited was rich in all kinds of vegetation on which they could feed. No scientist has ever given a satisfactory explanation for their disappearance—that is, from the viewpoint of evolution.

Not only reptiles but also a host of other peculiar animals lived simultaneously with them, and they perished just as suddenly. The rocks contain literally hundreds of extinct types, and their extermination is a profound mystery to the geologists.

The Cretaceous is known as the time of the great submergence. All the continents were awash. Water spread great sheets of sediment from Alaska to Mexico. Masses of granitic materials, probably semimolten, had just thrust aloft in what is now the Rocky Mountain front. Farther west a great block 400 miles long and 100 miles wide tilted up on edge, forming the Sierra Nevada Mountains. Sediments washed off from the block filled the trough to the west of it with thousands of feet of sand and clay.

One problem has puzzled diluvialists and has caused evolutionists to ridicule the Flood theory of geology. How, they ask, could such a terrific volume of water sweep over the earth without mixing all kinds of life together in one grand jumble, without any order or system? But if we read the Genesis record carefully, we learn that it took 150 days—five months—before the waters reached the tops of the highest hills. Even though wave action may have been violent—and abundant evidence indicates that it was—the waters must have risen gradually, sweeping away zone after zone, habitat after habitat, and burying the plants and animals in mud and sand, thus producing the fossil zones that correspond roughly to the earth's original life zones.

Notice that I said "roughly." We must not conclude that the fossil zones now exist in exactly the same location as the original ones, or that they are perfect replicas of them. Because of the violent wave action, many of the specimens would have washed for long distances before coming to rest. Some mixing would, of course, occur. But the fact that we find any order or sequence at all indicates the existence of some definite arrangement in the original world.

The Genesis record of the Flood states that after the 150 days the waters decreased, and after that there followed another period of increased activity. The rocks show it plainly. It must have required a period of great wave activity to lay down the thousands of feet of sediments. While we find evidence of great distur-bances during this period—the sediments' containing many breaks—there appears to have been a later extremely violent period that involved not only water action but the crust of the earth itself. In many places the strata were highly tilted or overturned, sometimes thrust laterally over lower strata. In the Banff region of Alberta, for instance, tremendous geological forces have tilted six great mountain blocks and shoved one over the other. The tourist can see most of them from one viewpoint beside the highway west of Banff village.

Uniformitarians and diluvialists alike have been at a loss to account for such tremendous earth movements. J. S. Lee of the University of Peking, in his *Geology of China,* has suggested that irregularities in the rotation of the earth, which would set up stresses in the rocks, caused them.

The great Rift Valley of Africa shows perhaps the most visually spectacular of the earth's movements. A great crack, as it were, on the earth's surface, it runs for a distance of 4,000 miles, from Palestine through the Red Sea and into the lake region of central Africa. The bottom of the Red Sea, part of the trough, lies 7,500 feet below sea level. Lake Tanganyika is nearly 4,200 feet deep, and cliffs bordering it rise 4,000 feet above its surface.

The rift is a notable example of shattering on a worldwide scale, involving the crust of the earth in its whole thickness. Some have described it as a virtual rending asunder of the earth's surface. Perhaps no other geological feature gives such clear evidence of a sudden and catastrophic movement, capable of tearing the earth apart along approximately one sixth of its circumference. It was, as the famous geologist Suess once remarked, "the breaking up of the terrestrial globe."

Not only is there the great Rift Valley, but a number of smaller rifts have formed, resembling the African valley in all respects except for magnitude. Recent studies have discovered similar features in the centers of the Atlantic, Indian, and Pacific oceans. They are connected with what geologists call plate tectonics, or continental drift.

Several years ago Alfred Wegener, a German geophysicist and meteorologist, suggested that the continents had not always been in their present positions, but they had drifted apart. North America could be fitted against Europe, South America against Africa, and Australia against southern Asia and Africa. The notion received much ridicule, but a number of scientists began to investigate the theory. The result has been that quite recently most geologists are accepting the idea.

The outer shell of the earth consists, the theory says, of a number of rigid plates, each moving independently on the plastic substance of the mantle and coming into collision with other plates. Where two plates meet horizontally relative to each other, mountains are thrust up. In other areas the plates shove each other down, one beneath the other, producing deep trenches in the sea bottom.

According to the evolutionary concept it would take 100,000,000 years to make an ocean basin or a mountain range.

Recent observations along the Mid-Atlantic Ridge

and other areas on the ocean bottoms indicate a spreading and that molten material is continually being injected between the two plates. As it comes out into the water it forms what geologists call pillow lavas. A report in the *National Geographic* of August, 1976, tells of exploration in the Cayman Trench in the Caribbean. The trench is 23,000 feet deep. A deep-sea submersible vessel has penetrated to 12,000 feet and has made important observations on the soft material of the mantle on which the crust rides.

If movement actually does take place, it introduces a difficult problem. What could cause a slow spreading of not more than a few inches a year? A number of theories have attempted to explain it. Certainly diluvialists cannot accept any theory that would involve millions of years. If it has taken place to any great degree, as geologists generally believe, diluvialists would have to place it within the actions of the Flood.

In describing the beginning of the Flood, the Bible says that all the fountains of the great deep broke up. The word used here for "broken up" occurs in Zechariah 14:4 to refer to the cleaving apart of the Mount of Olives when the Lord descends upon it. Again in Numbers 16:31, when the earth swallowed up Korah, Dathan, and Abiram, it cleaved apart—the same word. Evidently when the Flood started, there occurred great tectonic movements. But according to the geological evidence, the greatest movements took place in the latter portion of the Flood, after the great masses of sedimentary rocks had been laid down. Apparently this correlates with the situation that exists between the rocks of North America and Europe, which have a close resemblance, as if they were once connected.

The apparent connection between the rocks of the two continents has long puzzled scientists, as it has been difficult to imagine how erosion could have created such a gulf between them. It may be that the theory of continental drift is the answer.

Diluvialists can accept the plate tectonics theory without fearing any inconsistency with their Creation theory as long as it is placed within the actions of the great Genesis Flood.

Chapter 6

Water, Fire, and Ice

The rocks above the Cretaceous are much more difficult to decipher than those lower down. It seems that
at about this stage of deposition, great mountain
ranges were forced up. Later sediments were less extensive and were deposited in between the uplifts, in
what might be called inter-mountain basins.

The next series above the Cretaceous is known as
the Tertiary. Not all of these rocks, however, were in
the basins between the mountain masses. Extensive
Tertiary deposits were spread out above the flat-lying
strata of the plains east of the present Rockies or on the
rocks of the Texas coastal plain.

Geologists have labeled the Tertiary rocks the "Age
of Mammals" because paleontologists have found most
of the mammals in them. Some of the smaller forms,
such as shrews and moles, which burrow in the
ground, appear as far down as the Triassic. But the
larger animals evidently escaped the rising waters until
the last.

Tertiary rocks are divided into five parts (reading
from the bottom upward): Paleocene, Eocene,
Oligocene, Miocene, and Pliocene. Each mass of Ter-

tiary rock receives its name from its fossil content. Since geologists have done this according to the evolutionary scheme, we may find it difficult at times to make any correlation between the strata and events of the Flood. Therefore we must pass over them lightly, but we'll mention a few important points.

One difficult question to answer is when the Flood action ceased. Evidence suggests that there was a long period—possibly hundreds of years—after Noah came out of the ark during which the earth was still greatly unsettled. Some mountain ranges built up through volcanic action, and rock movements on a large scale appear to have taken place.

About the only clue we can get as to when the earth became more or less stable is by studying the fossils in the Tertiary rocks. In the lower portions most of the mammals are of extinct types. But when we get to the Miocene there appears to be a change, and in the Pliocene many are like modern types. It is about as close as we can come to an approximation of the closing events of the Flood.

One of the outstanding phenomena of the upper strata is the tremendous amount of igneous rocks. The action is of two kinds: (1) explosive, with ashes and steam blown violently from a crater, and (2) effusive, in which lavas flow quietly, either from craters or from fissures.

In the Canadian Shield, the rocks have been cracked and broken, and a large amount of igneous material extruded. About 20,000 cubic miles of this extrusive material poured out in the Lake Superior region alone. Much of it has hardened into granitic rocks.

Water, Fire, and Ice

The western highlands of the United States and the Appalachians have about 75,000 square miles covered with such material. A similar area in the great Columbia Plateau, involving much of eastern Oregon and Washington, part of Idaho, and other nearby states extends over 200,000 square miles. Here the lavas are from 1,500 to 7,000 feet deep, having buried whole mountains beneath them. Most of the material came up through fissures. The only large volcanic cones are along the Cascades on the western edge of the region, though some smaller ones appear here and there. One of the most spectacular portions of the region is in the Craters of the Moon National Monument, in eastern Idaho, where the whole surface of the ground is a mass of black lava, broken and irregular, with some spatter cones.

The activity of the Columbia Plateau must have begun early, at least on the western side, for the lavas mingle with sediments from the bottom to the top. Volcanic activity continued after the depositing of most of the sediments, for layers of lava cover much of the area.

In India the Deccan Plateau measures 200,000 square miles, and Argentina has another lava flow of 300,000 square miles. Both areas resemble the Columbia Plateau.

The sedimentary deposits on the Great Plains west of the Mississippi River include much volcanic ash. In Nebraska the gravels mingle with volcanic ash belched from craters hundreds of miles away. Many of the scattered basins in the Rocky Mountain region contain volcanic materials blown out into water. The Coast

Ranges of California consist largely of volcanic materials, some from craters and some from fissures.

Perhaps the most outstanding evidences of violent volcanism occur in South Africa. Du Toit's *Geology of South Africa* says that lavas poured out beneath water and mingled with sedimentary material. Afterward came the extrusion of granites and other igneous rocks. When the material had hardened, the beds tilted, and more molten material flowed over them. The process repeated itself again and again. Whole masses of rock miles in diameter broke away and floated off upon the molten mass, which spread out and formed immense sheets of granite.

Some areas domed up, turned over, and instantly metamorphosed. Volcanic explosions took place through the deposits. Then geologic forces again elevated and folded the rock layers, and great quantities of pebbles were swept off toward the south, forming huge deltas. Afterward, more rivers of lava poured out, forming masses 1,000 to 4,000 feet thick. Further foldings occurred.

It is difficult to comprehend the magnitude of such geological actions, but it is easy to recognize that terrific violence must have broken up the entire crust of the earth. Intense volcanism must have taken place simultaneously with crustal movements and water action.

Closely related is another phenomenon called magmatic uplift. Geologists believe that some of the mantle of the earth is, or has been, partly melted. Or it may be that the weight of the rocks keeps portions of the mantle in a semimolten state, and the breakup might allow it to escape, as in the bottom of the Mid-Atlantic Ridge, where we have plain proof that such movement is taking place. It may be that the terrific tectonic movements have had a part in creating this situation. While some of the material found itself forced up through fissures, in other places great uplifts resulted in what geologists call batholiths. A batholithic movement elevated the Rocky Mountain chain. In western Idaho is the Idaho batholith, which uplifted great masses of rock. The Black Hills of South Dakota domed up, and the overlying sediments washed off the top of the dome. Many other great mountain masses formed the same way.

Not only volcanism, with its lava flows and the magmatic masses, transformed the face of the earth after the Flood, but so did what geologists call the Glacial Period. Although they say that the period occurred from 25,000 to 100,000 years ago, it is possible to place it in a much shorter period of time after the Flood. It is a natural consequence of the Flood events and of the volcanism that followed.

What could have brought on the Glacial Period after the Flood? Many scientists believe that volcanic activity had the greatest influence in triggering a glacial age. William J. Humphrey, one-time professor of Meteorological Physics, United States Weather Bureau, advanced the theory some years ago. The water vapor, carbon dioxide, and dust in the atmosphere reduce the sun's radiation. Dust has two effects: It both absorbs and reflects the sun's heat. After the great eruption of Krakatoa in the East Indies in 1883 and of Katmai in Alaska in 1912, a large amount of dust continued to float in the upper atmosphere. Such a shell of volcanic dust is thirty times more effective in shutting out the sun's rays than it is in holding in the heat from the earth. Scientists call it the reverse greenhouse effect. A greenhouse lets the sunlight in but keeps the heat from escaping. The same thing happens in a closed car. But the reverse effect of dust would result in a greatly lowered temperature on the surface of the earth.

When we look for remnants of ancient volcanoes in western North America we find a line extending practically the whole length of the continent. Of course if we look at them in terms of millions of years of activity, it would not mean much. However, if we think in the framework of the Flood and a comparatively short time during which the volcanoes were in action, we can see that the effect would be tremendous.

It is not hard to imagine their impact when they were erupting by the hundreds. The snow line would be lower in the mountains, but in the valleys conditions might be suitable for habitation close to the snow line. Scientists have estimated that the average annual temperature need lower only a few degrees to bring on a great accumulation of ice and snow, provided there was enough moisture, as would have been the case after the Flood.

As the earth emerged from the Flood, every interior basin would have been full. Such areas now occupy about one fifth of the land surface of the earth. Great regions that are now desert, such as the Great Basin, the Caspian Basin, and parts of the Sahara would have been vast lakes. In addition, thousands of lakes existed that have drained away. The whole world must have had a humid climate. The air would have been heavy with moisture, not only from the evaporation of water from inland basins and lakes but also from volcanic eruptions, since they throw great volumes of steam into the air.

Under such conditions certain areas of the earth's surface would experience the condensation of immense quantities of atmospheric vapor in the form of rain and snow.

Some diluvialists have tried to limit the ice action to masses of drift ice washed about by the Flood. But while we might be able to explain a few glacial phenomena by floating ice, we cannot do so for most of them. The evidence is clear that there were large masses of ice in northeastern North America and northern Europe.

First, there are the polished rocks. Anyone who has been in the high mountains and observed the rocks below a glacier can readily distinguish between ice polish and water polish. As a glacier moves, it drags along on its under surface masses of sand and gravel that act as scouring agents. Furthermore, ice will plane off rough surfaces, leaving depressions untouched, in contrast with water, which smoothes all surfaces alike. The sand and gravel beneath the ice, as they travel along, will leave scratches, or striae. The glacier will deposit masses of boulders and broken rock fragments in moraines along its sides and at its melting front. Geologists call the boulders erratics, because they are different from the underlying rock the glacier dropped them on.

Streams flowing beneath the ice may accumulate

gravel and sand along the bottoms of the channels through which they flow. When the ice melts, the debris will remain as mounds or long winding hills known as eskers. They are common in the northeastern states and in Canada.

We can plainly see glacial evidences not only in the mountains and in Alaska, where large glaciers are common, but also over the entire area where the great ice mass once existed. If we go to the Missouri River from the west or to the Ohio from the south, we find none of the features until we cross the rivers. But as soon as we do, we will find glacial phenomena everywhere. All of New England has them, and we may see them in a line from New York to the Ohio.

In the Alps and in the Sierra Nevadas, evidences of ice action occur far below the present levels. In Yosemite National Park, for instance, the Lyell Glacier lies at 12,000 feet, but one can trace its former course down the valleys to about 4,000 feet. At Tenaya Lake (8,100 feet) boulders lie in great profusion. One finds polished granite and great moraines in which debris dropped when the ice melted.

Most geologists claim successive periods of glaciation during geological time. Mingled with the stratified rocks are certain deposits called tillites, made up of a mixture of fine and coarse materials that resemble glacial debris. But the evidence is not conclusive, and geologists admit that the question is one of great perplexity. Terrific floods of water could produce many of the phenomena. When one finds supposed glacial evidences in equatorial regions, they raise a serious problem.

Water, Fire, and Ice

Geologists designate the Glacial Period in the geological column as Pleistocene. They divide it into four stages. In America they are: Kansan, Nebraskan, Illinoian, and Wisconsin. Whether they are all true glacial stages or variations in one major glacial action is not clear. Some good authorities have stated that the lower stages are nothing but outwash from the Wisconsin stage of the ice.

In certain places we find beds of clay deposited by glacial ice. The layers, known as varves, contain both coarse and fine layers. Similar layers occur in some glacial lakes today, as at Lake Louise in the Canadian Rockies. During the summer the fine mud brought down by the streams from the glaciers above, which the ice has worn off the rocks beneath, is coarser and thicker than in the winter layers. This annual layer, or varve, geologists take as a guide to the ancient varves, which they also assume to be annual. On this basis they reckon the length of time for the deposition of the glacial clays. Geologists thus estimate that it took 10,000 years for the ice to melt back from Connecticut to Canada.

Clearly the creationist will find such dating objectionable and will inquire if it is reliable. Interestingly, some authorities on glaciation question the method's accuracy. They say that the ice mass melted simultaneously over the whole region.

Melting of glacial ice is not the only process that could have produced varves. One investigator in Denmark found that during the summer a series of fluctuations had created varves that previous studies had mistaken for annual deposits, and that four hundred varves from a certain locality had formed in twenty years. It would seem that such a method of dating glacial movements is too undependable to be of much value.

We should also point out that if the glaciation came after the Flood, much debris would already lie scattered over the earth. In glaciated regions the ice would rework it. The glaciers may not have done so much actual carving as we have sometimes credited them with.

After studying all the evidences for glaciation, we come to the conclusion that they fall into three classes: (1) those that ice *must* have produced, (2) those that water *must* have done, and (3) those that either or both *may* have accomplished. In general, they are easy to correlate with the Flood theory of geology.

We have now reviewed the various lines of evidence from the rocks that we can show to correlate with the Genesis record of the Flood. The nature of the stratified rocks indicates deposition under conditions of such violence that it is almost impossible to give an adequate concept of their magnitude. Volcanism on an incomprehensible scale has affected much of the earth's surface. Gigantic tectonic movements have moved mountains out of their places, overturned them, and made great rifts. Erosion by water, wind, and ice has carved the uplifted and folded rocks into jagged peaks and fantastic shapes. At the same time great fields of ice and snow have left their imprints. How true was God's declaration: "I will destroy man . . . from the face of the earth" (Genesis 6:7). The Bible record of the Flood has a sound scientific foundation, and geological phenomena, when correctly understood, act as powerful witnesses to the truthfulness of the Bible story.

Chapter 7

Stone Age Man

One of the most intriguing of all geological puzzles is that of prehistoric man. Today anthropologists are working diligently to make a coordinated picture of the origin and ascent of man from primitive apelike creatures to the present human race.

The Great Chain of Being was a philosophic line of thought that dominated theology during the medieval period. In the eighteenth century it held much the same position that evolution did in the nineteenth and twentieth centuries. Principally the concept concerned man's position in nature. Under its influence scholars became obsessed with the idea of filling all the missing links in the chain, particularly those leading to man. The science of anthropology arose out of such interests.

Buffon spoke in 1749 of man's similarity to the apes. Lamarck in 1809 declared that man had descended from them. During the early nineteenth century, interest was at a fever pitch, and anthropologists looked for any evidence regarding man's ancestry.

In 1823 a primitive-appearing skull was discovered at Engis, France, and another at Gibraltar in 1848. By the middle of the century many evidences of ancient

97

cave life had turned up in France and Belgium, and in 1863 Charles Lyell wrote a monograph entitled *Geological Evidences of the Antiquity of Man*. Fragments of a human skeleton unearthed in a cave in the Neanderthal (Neander Valley) in Germany in 1856 and named Neanderthal man aroused great hope that at last science had found the missing link.

At one time the glaciers of the Alps extended as much as forty or more miles below their present terminations. The rivers stood from one hundred to two hundred feet above current levels. Large amounts of gravel brought down from the ends of the glaciers formed terraces along the rivers. Evidences of human occupation appeared in the lower terraces, and in addition many caves had formed in the limestone cliffs along the rivers. The caves also contained signs of human occupancy. Their inhabitants had built fires at the cave mouths, and the caves had apparently protected them from the weather and from wild beasts.

Ancient man made ice-age shelters by stretching skins over poles and then using mammoth bones to hold them in place. Inside the shelters they constructed hearths of mammoth bones. Archaeologists have found bones, both from the outside and the inside, in large numbers.

Since the discovery of the first specimen of Neanderthal man, anthropologists have unearthed about one hundred others, all of them fragmentary. But a few were complete enough to give a good idea of the anatomy of the race. Neanderthals lived all the way from Belgium to Iraq and into northern Africa.

Neanderthal man was short and robust, with a

small cranium and limb bones much like those of modern man. The arms were short and the fingers stubby. An unusual feature of the skull were the prominent ridges over the eyes. In spite of many illustrations showing him as stooped, science now knows that his posture was upright. As anthropologists obtained more and more specimens, it became apparent that the being was not a link between man and the apes but simply a variant in man himself. Anthropologists now believe that the so called "primitive" features were aberrations from the normal, and do not indicate any relation to the lower animals. Some have said that if a Neanderthal were to dress in modern clothes, he could pass down the city streets without anyone's noticing him.

What happened to the Neanderthals we do not know. Whether later invaders of Europe exterminated them, or they gradually died out, we can only conjecture.

As it began to be evident that Neanderthal man offered no solution to the ancestry of man, interest turned elsewhere. A Dutch anatomy professor, Eugène Dubois, resigned his position and joined the Royal Dutch East Indian Army, hoping to have an opportunity to excavate in the Far East. The colonial authorities allowed him to dig in Java, and in 1894 he announced the discovery of a skullcap, teeth, and a thigh bone, which he pieced together and named *Pithecanthropus erectus*—the erect ape-man.

The skullcap was small and had a distinctly simian appearance. Much discussion arose as to whether it was a gibbon or a primitive man. For thirty years

Dubois refused to allow anyone to see the specimen. All scientists had to study were the plaster casts he gave them. The femur was distinctly human.

During the years after the discovery of *Pithecan-thropus* many more bones of primitive creatures—no one knew whether apes or men—continued to come to light in southeast Asia. The classification became more and more confused. The Geological Survey of China and the Rockefeller Foundation kept from fifty to one hundred men working in the area near Peking for ten years in search of specimens. The remains they found received the name *Sinanthropus*—China man. Anthropologists advanced many theories about the relation of the fossils to the modern Chinese, but none of them have proved to be of much value in solving the problem of man's origin.

About the time the discussion over the Asian specimens reached its height, a discovery in South Africa turned attention in another direction. In 1924 Raymond Dart, of the University of Johannesburg, found a skull near Kimberly. It appeared to be that of a child about six years old. He named it *Australopithecus africanus*—southern Africa ape. The specimen consisted of part of a skull with a slanting forehead and low cranium. The face looked like that of a chimpanzee. Other features were more human, and from the shape of the occipital bones a number of scientists believed that the creature had been able to walk upright.

Anthropologists have not yet been able to agree as to whether it was an ape or a hominid—a creature on the way to becoming human. Later exploration revealed many more specimens, mostly scattered fragments and a large number of teeth.

In spite of the difficulties in the way of deciding what *Australopithecus* really was, another twenty-five years saw it generally accepted as probably the oldest example of a hominid. Other specimens found in the same area, but having a more modern appearance, acquired the name *Homo erectus,* which was supposed to be a little closer to modern man. But what about the Asiatic specimens? Scientists have since classified most of them as *Homo erectus.*

Physical anthropology now struggled with the question, "Did humanity have only one origin, or did it have two, one in Asia and one in Africa?"

And what did the creationists have to say about the situation? Not much. Some of them thought that *Australopithecus* was an ape, not a human, but others saw in him a degenerate type of humanity. They have reached no general agreement as yet.

The complacency of the anthropologists regarding the origin of man vanished when in 1959 Dr. and Mrs. Louis Leakey, working in the Olduvai Gorge in Tanzania, discovered bones that they named *Zinjanthropus*—East African man. Leakey, curator of the National Museum at Nairobi, Kenya, firmly believed that man had originated in Africa. He selected Olduvai Gorge, an eroded lake bed, as the best site for exploration. For thirty years he and his wife, digging at different levels, found many evidences of human occupancy but never a human specimen.

Mary Leakey was a digging expert as well as her husband. On a hot July day in 1959 Leakey was ill in his tent, and Mary was searching on one of the levels in the gorge. Suddenly she saw what looked like human teeth. She brushed away the soil and exposed a jaw-bone and teeth. Jumping up, she rushed back to the tent, exclaiming, "I found a man." Her husband leaped out of bed, and forgetting his illness, dressed and hurried out to see what she had discovered. Then he set his crew to work, and eventually they unearthed over four hundred fragments of bone. When assembled they made a peculiar-appearing skull. It had a high face, with a sharply sloping forehead and large browridges. Although flat like that of a gorilla, in other ways it resembled a human. The teeth of the upper jaw were like those of *Australopithecus.* They did not find the lower jaw.

Leakey sent samples of the soil in which they found the skull to New York for potassium-argon tests, which dated at 1,750,000 years. The results seemed to confirm Leakey's estimate that the skull was the oldest human ever found. But most anthropologists reacted in shock when they heard of the date. It was about a million years older than any known human fossil had been dated. If it was man, how could he have existed so far beyond *Australopithecus,* from which man supposedly descended?

Further work revealed another modern-appearing skull and other bones, which Leakey named *Homo habilis.* It was in the same layer as *Zinjanthropus* and a few feet lower. Now the anthropologists had not just one type, but three types of primitive hominids, and they were in a quandary as to how to interpret them. Spirited discussions followed, and eventually they reached a decision. The specimens were all variants of

Australopithecus. And so the problem seemed solved.

But it did not rest long. Leakey's son Richard had been working near Lake Rudolf in northern Kenya. There his crews had uncovered many bones of australopithecines. On one of his trips to the excavation site a workman handed Richard a bag of bone fragments, which he took back to his headquarters. The work crews unearthed more bones from the same site, and after six weeks he and his wife assembled them into a complete skull. The skull, when they announced its discovery, sent more shocks of dismay through the anthropological world. Known only by its museum number "1470," the skull has a distinctly modern appearance. Tests on the soil gave an age of nearly 3,000,000 years. But the most disconcerting aspect of the find was that many specimens of *Australopithecus* had turned up in the same area. Also Leakey found some specimens that he classed as "advanced." Here were all three types of hominids or what-have-you, all together.

Richard lectured in London and in New York, and his reception was not always cordial. Many were skeptical of his interpretation of his "1470" skull. But he maintained his position, declaring that they would either have to throw out the skull or discard their theories on the course of man's ascent.

Time, November 7, 1977, graphically portrayed the whole problem. The article referred to discoveries made many years ago in the Siwalik Hills of India, where paleontologists had excavated ape bones from the Tertiary rocks. Among them was one ape named *Ramapithecus*. When the problem regarding the australopithecines arose, anthropologists remembered that *Ramapithecus* had once led to suggestions regarding its relation to mankind. Since its first discovery paleontologists had found at least forty specimens, and twenty-four of them had been described in detail.

In 1961 Leakey had found a skull of an ape named *Kenyapithecus*. Now some decided that it and *Ramapithecus* were the same. Paleontologists have located the genus in India, East Africa, and Asia Minor, and the specimens are all similar to what Leakey had called *Proconsul*. Physical anthropology revised the theory of man's ascent and declared *Ramapithecus* to be the true ancestor of both man and the higher apes. The decision rested on the fact that he had in his skull fragments and in the teeth slightly closer resemblances to modern man than did any of the other ape genera yet known.

The various species of *Ramapithecus* have been dated all the way from 14,000,000 years ago down to 4,000,000 years, still leaving a big gap between them and the other hominids. Incidentally, the reader will recall that in a previous chapter we have shown why creationists do not accept such dates as valid.

Anthropological theory has had to make radical revisions, for if "1470" and the australopithecines lived together 3,000,000 years ago, the latter could not have been the ancestor of modern man.

British anthropologist Chris C. Hummer published a critical analysis of the evidence for *Ramapithecus* as an ancestor of man, in the *Creation Research Society Quarterly* of September, 1978. *Ramapithecus*, he says, is the only current candidate for being the first member of the human family. But his theory faces many problems. In the first place, a huge gap exists between the accepted dates for *Pithecanthropus* and *Ramapithecus*—around four million years. Then we have the fact that while we find *Ramapithecus* fossils in many countries—the major ones in India, Kenya, Hungary, Greece, Turkey, and Pakistan—they supposedly gave rise to later forms only in Africa.

All of the major ramapithecine fragments consist only of teeth and pieces of jaws that would hardly fill a cigar box. We have no postcranial bones. It is impossible, anthropologists declare, to tell much about the life habits from such meager materials. Several authorities state emphatically that the evidence is not sufficient to warrant placing *Ramapithecus* as the ancestor of hominids.

Hummer feels that one cannot overemphasize the importance of *Ramapithecus*. If it is not accepted, a gap of 20,000 million years, according to evolutionary thinking, falls between any other possible ancestor and man.

Donald Carl Johanson made another spectacular discovery in Ethiopia. On high, bare cliffs and weathered ridges he discovered 40 percent of a complete skeleton. The palate still had sixteen teeth in place. Johanson and his staff named the skeleton "Lucy." They uncovered many other specimens until they had what they considered to be a whole family group, from a baby to adults. The creatures were similar to modern man, not to the australopithecines, and were dated at 2.6 million years.

Now we will return to the situation in Europe.

Three skulls—Swanscome, Steinheim, and Fontéchevade—have thrown light on the meaning of the Neanderthal specimens. The Swanscome skull turned up in Thames gravels, associated with artifacts older than those of Neanderthal. The Steinheim skull, found in Germany, was a typical Caucasoid, and somewhat modern in appearance. Early tools accompanied it.

The most interesting find was the one at Fontéchevade, France. In a cave, superficial layers yielded typical Neanderthal artifacts, below which lay a hard, limy crust that seemed to be the bottom of the cave. But when they pierced it, the excavators encountered more than twenty feet of deposits. At a depth of eight feet were animal bones, stone tools, and fragments of a skull. Tests showed that the bones were older than Neanderthal bones. When assembled, the fragments proved to be of modern type. The general conclusion has been that all the finds indicated a superior pre-Neanderthal race.

Excavations in Palestine have revealed specimens that show a slight tendency toward Neanderthal features. Anthropologists can trace them across Europe. It seems evident that early migrations brought the fairly "modern"-appearing men into Europe, where they deteriorated into the typical Neanderthals.

Some have suggested that their anatomical peculiarities resulted from two factors—climate and inbreeding. To those we might add poor nutrition. As man spread over the earth after the Flood, he would not always be able to find suitable food. Evidences from ancient sites indicate that he ate anything he could lay his hands on, from insects, shellfish, amphibians, to wild cattle, horses, and elephants. It would be somewhat difficult to obtain a balanced diet from such materials, and without doubt lack of proper nutrition would result in deterioration.

Disease would also cause deformity. In a large hospital I once saw a young person of about eighteen years of age whose facial features were so distorted that the profile was a perfect image of a typical Neanderthal. Not many years ago two anatomists examined the skeletons of some of the Neanderthals that had served as the basis for the earlier reconstructions, and they pronounced them "rotten with arthritis."

Some evidence suggests that as soon as early man settled down to cultivate vegetables, grains, and fruits, the physical features improved rapidly. It was not the result of evolution. In fact, anthropologists remark that the change was too rapid to be accounted for by evolutionary processes. Rather, it was a natural result of improved nutrition and living conditions.

What we have said of Neanderthal we may apply with equal validity to other primitive races. If we go back to the Bible record of the dispersion of man from one central region—the Mesopotamian valleys—we may readily account for the presence of "primitive"— really deteriorated—men around the perimeter of their spread, into Europe, Africa, and Asia. The evidence is as fully valid for such a viewpoint as it is for the evolution of man from apelike creatures millions of years ago.

Sherwood L. Washburn, professor of physical anthropology at the University of California in Berkeley, critically discussed the problems surrounding the interpretation of the evidence of human evolution in the September, 1978, *Scientific American*. He said that anthropologists disagree on many points regarding the significance of many of the specimens. Physical anthropology has no clearly defined rules for comparing anatomical features or assigned dates. A high degree of emotion surrounds the whole subject. Some of the questions under study for many years still remain unanswered, and facts differ so widely as to reliability that all current theories may prove to be wrong. Anthropology must make more discoveries before it can settle the vital problems of man's origin.

The question arises about archaeology in America. Was there a similar development to that in the Old World? In answer we may say that explorations in American caves and terraces have not been as fruitful as in Europe, yet a few discoveries help us to understand something about our country's early inhabitants. Recently archaeology in America has undergone a boom. Archaeologists are investigating many sites before urban development makes them inaccessible. The correlation of sites in America with those of Europe is difficult, but a study of river terraces in Oregon indicates a history probably parallel to that in Europe. Alluvial deposits occur along the margins of the Willamette Valley and many smaller valleys, sloping from 1,000 feet down to 300 feet. On top of the slopes are terraces that have spread out from the canyons.

A summary of the evidences of human habitation in America would lead one to conclude that for several hundred years, perhaps for 2,000 years or more after the Flood, glacial conditions prevailed in the north and in the mountains. Man lived here during that time. Some investigators have placed the latest date for the glaciation as late as 500 BC.

The animal life of the American glacial period was quite different from that of the present. Camels, wild horses, reindeer, bison, elephants, mammoths, ground sloths, and bears now extinct roamed the land. Mastodon and mammoth bones are found on top of the latest glacial deposits in Indiana and Ohio.

Evidences of man are not as frequent as in Europe. A few cases reach back into glacial time, but few American finds have proved to be "primitive." Neanderthaloid bones have turned up in Patagonia, Chile, Bolivia, and a few in North America. Most of the North American aborigines seem to have been of Mongolian type.

The most important work done on North American archaeology is that at the Koster dig, a few miles north of the Illinois town of Kampsville. It is one of the biggest prehistoric Indian sites in all of North America. Archaeologists have recognized fifteen levels, representing different eras of occupation. They date the levels back to at least 6,000 BC.

Those working at Koster estimate their excavations have uncovered not more than 10 percent of the prehistoric village, yet the materials unearthed are tremendous. They have found over 19,000 artifacts of bone, stone, shell, iron, and copper, plus several million specimens of animal remains, and 600,000 of plant materials.

Carbon-14 dates give ages of from 5,000 to 6,000

years (carbon-14 years, remember), and they reveal a civilization much more sophisticated than we have generally recognized as existing so far back. The evidences here tie in well with those from other parts of the world in suggesting that early man was not a crude savage but an intelligent, capable individual.

Chapter 8

Cavemen
and
City Sites

During the early nineteenth century, because of the extensive road building in central Europe, workmen often ran across evidences of former human habitation, such as fragments of bone, stone implements, and other artifacts. Boucher de Perthes, a customs official, became interested, and in 1838 he published a monograph on them.

About the same time, explorations in the caves in the limestone rocks along the rivers and old campsites in the gravel revealed hearths, smoke-covered cave ceilings, and other signs of ancient civilization. In 1830 the Danish government created a commission to study the refuse heaps and shell mounds common in that country. The Royal Museum made a collection, and Christian Thomsen, their curator, developed a chronology. Since most of the sites had in them some kind of stone implements, and many of them had bronze and iron, he divided the stages of human culture into three parts—Stone Age, Bronze Age, and Iron Age. Further explorations in Belgium, France, and Germany revealed many more cave dwellings and many sites along the gravel terraces of the rivers.

The gravels along the rivers in France lie in two levels. The lower level was deposited before the onset of the ice, and the high level on the outwash from the glaciers. The presence of artifacts on some of the lower levels indicates that man had already come into the region before the ice had reached its lowest level. But most of the discoveries took place in the limestone caves. As an illustration we might notice the deposits found in a cave at Castillo, Spain. Forty-five feet of materials on the floor showed the following (layers are numbered from the bottom up):

13. Dagger of copper
12. Flint implements
11. Engravings on a staghorn
10. Flints, engravings, reindeer horn
9-6. Reindeer bones
5-4. Stone implements
3. Stone and flint implements
2. Bones of the cave bear and hyena
1. Crude flint implements

Here we see that the lower part of the cave deposit had the Old Stone Age implements, while higher up there appeared carvings on bone, and then copper artifacts. The Castillo cave was typical of many others. One at Le Mas d'Azil in southern France contained the following sequence:

9. Gallo-Roman remains of iron, glass, and pottery
8. Pottery, stone implements, copper and bronze
7. Pottery and flint
6. Flints, harpoon of bone
5. Sterile level
4. Harpoons of bone and engravings on bone

3. Sterile river-flood layer
2. Harpoons of bone, flint and bone implements
1. Gravel with fire hearths

The French cave has more bone and metal artifacts than the other one.

As archaeologists excavated many of the caves, the sequence of stone, bronze, and iron became clear. It is evident that mankind occupied them from their first entrance into the country until bronze and iron indicated Roman times. Of course it does not mean that the caves were the only places where men lived. They might have been used even after man built better homes.

Archaeologists divided the Stone Age—Paleolithic—into four divisions of main importance, and later into eight. The first scheme will suffice to illustrate the development of cultures, and so we will not go into more detail. The lowest and most crudely formed implements found were Chellean, first found at Chelles, France. The banks of the Marne contained flints of simple structure mingled with bones of the hippopotamus, rhinoceros, elephant, giant beaver, and hyena. Plant remains indicate a forest much like that of the present.

At Saint-Acheul, on the Somme, were terraces with flints of a better grade, and from that site came the name of the Acheulian culture. Similar finds showed up in other parts of France and in England.

Archaeologists unearthed the most prominent remains of the Paleolithic period at Le Moustier in central France. They were associated with Neanderthal man. From that site archaeologists established the Mousterian culture. Then in many places, immediately above the Mousterian, appeared the remains of another race, the Cro-Magnons. Well-built, much like modern man in appearance, they replaced the Neanderthals, apparently without mingling with them. Their culture received the name Aurignacian.

One of the most outstanding records of the Aurignacian culture occurs in the artwork on walls of caves and on fragments of bones and horn. The Cro-Magnon people made drawings, often in brilliant colors, of woolly mammoths, cave bears, bison, reindeer, lions, horses, fish, cattle, and stags. They made carvings of many of the animals and of human figures on horn, tusks, and bone. Altogether they were a highly artistic race.

We do not know why they made the paintings and carvings. Some have thought that it might have been part of their religious activity, such as drawing pictures as hunting charms. After prolonged study of the works of the Cro-Magnons, one cannot avoid the conclusions that their capacity was nearly if not as high as our own; that they were capable of advanced education; that they had a strongly developed aesthetic as well as religious sense; that their society was quite highly differentiated along the lines of talent for work in different kinds.

The Neanderthals disappeared without leaving any evidence of a permanent heritage. But the Cro-Magnons may have merged with later migrants into central Europe and contributed to their development. Some authorities have suggested that traces of their lineage may linger in the fringe of western Europe, such as the Bretons of France, the Irish, and the highland Scotch.

We have cited a few illustrations of early life in Europe to show that the evidence is for migration of one group after another, rather than for evolution of one from the other. The higher grade of tools in the upper levels of the caves seems to show that they came in with new groups rather than resulted from the evolving skills of the early habitants.

Colin Renfrew gave an interesting comment on the history of some of the early European men in the November, 1977, *National Geographic*. He said that many have abandoned the idea that the people of central Europe received all their civilization from Mesopotamia. European farmers had discovered copper metallury before the Romans. Some of their temples they constructed before the pyramids in Egypt.

We will now go to the Middle East and see what we can learn about the development of early civilization there.

In upper Egypt four river terraces contain lower and middle Paleolithic implements. Archaeologists have traced the terraces for hundreds of miles. In lower Egypt Mousterian implements occur along the shores of the ancient lakes and on ocean beaches. The following data come from a report of the University of Chicago Institute explorations:

As the country emerged into its present geographical form it was a land of copious rainfall. Forest and grassland covered the hills surrounding the valley. Herds of wild animals roamed everywhere. The Nile alluvium is full of shells and bone and flint implements that cover the greater part of the floor of the basin, indicating that the plain was originally a swamp or a lake. Implements of lower Paleolithic types are abundant. Early man preferred the edges of the valley, which are now desert. The silt along the river bottom contains no stone implements, since it was laid down on mud flats. Man came into the valley before the river had eroded the mud flats down to their present level.

Egyptian urban culture began with the Neolithic— "New Stone Age." A culture that used copper immediately succeeded it. No evidence exists that the cities of the plain ever went through any Paleolithic stages.

What we have said of Egypt can also apply to Greece. It began with the Neolithic and copper cultures. Archaeologists have traced the same kinds of implements as far south as Uganda, Kenya, and Rhodesia.

Such facts correlate with the Flood theory of geology. The first migrants left crude implements, but as soon as they settled down and made better tools, they began to develop agriculture and to build cities.

Much the same story appears in the Middle East. Excavations in the Tigris and Euphrates valleys have revealed an intensely interesting situation. The first settlements occupied the Anatolian Plateau region in hills to the east of the valleys. The valleys were too marshy for settlement. But as soon as possible, migrations took place into the valleys from the north and east. In the upper Tigris Valley excavations at Tepe Gawra give one of the most complete sequences of cultural strata known.

The lowest level is Neolithic. The remains of the city

contain no Paleolithic implements, although archaeologists have found them scattered over the hills of the region. The implements were of flint and obsidian. The pottery was painted. Among the artifacts were axes, spears, arrowheads, chisels, needles, nails, hooks, bracelets, rings, toilet seats, and embossed ornaments.

Excavations at Ur, Abraham's city, revealed copper, gold, and gold and silver alloys. Writing existed, and the cities of the plain all showed well-constructed patterns of piers, columns, and walls. Some cities possessed cast copper and wheeled vehicles. A culture developed that used copper tools of a high degree of perfection.

Civilization here showed no sign of a long period of development. The earliest tombs of the kings of Ur contain gold instruments, beautifully decorated. Their craftsmen decorated chariots with red, white, and blue mosaic, with golden heads of lions having massive manes made of lapis lazuli, and with shell on the side panels. Among the other discoveries were gold heads of lions and bulls, silver lionesses, saws of gold, copper vessels—all beautifully done. The tombs they constructed of limestone slabs, whose nearest possible source was the hills thirty miles away.

At Catal Hüyük on the Anatolian Plateau north of the Taurus Mountains is one of the most extensive excavations made anywhere. The mound of the ancient city covered thirty-two acres. The buildings, made of sun-dried bricks, reeds, and plaster, with black mortar to hold them together, were constructed something like the multilevel pueblo dwellings of the New Mexico

Indians. They had no doorways, but the people entered them by ladders leading to the roofs. Paintings and sculpture adorned the interior walls.

Materials found in the ancient city indicate the presence of such industries as weaving, woodworking, and metalworking. Agriculture produced many kinds of grains and fruits as well as cattle and sheep. The people made many implements of stone and bone.

The whole site presents a picture of a well-developed civilization from the beginning. The materials were not native—the people carried on an extensive commerce with other areas.

In Palestine, as in Mesopotamia and Egypt, the earliest settlements occupied the hills while the valleys were yet too marshy. For many years archaeologists thought that Palestine and Mesopotamia had no Paleolithic cultures, but more recent explorations have shown evidence of nomads roaming the hills and using crude Stone Age implements.

Many believe Jericho to have been the first city ever built, although others question the idea. People apparently built early there because of its location in the deep valley of the Jordan River. A massive wall with round towers surrounded Jericho. Most of the stones of the wall came from the hills a mile away. Their tools consisted of flint, bone, and wood, and were of many varieties. Some served as knives; others, for cleaning skins. Farmers cut grain with sickle blades made by serrating stone edges with flint. The city's inhabitants also had agricultural and woodworking tools.

The houses were mostly of brick, with clay floors finished with lime plaster. The builders continued the floor surfacing on up the wall so that there were no sharp corners to collect dirt. They used reeds for the roofs.

Jericho carried on an extensive commerce with other cities, some materials coming from as far away as the shores of the Mediterranean. Apparently the inhabitants of Jericho obtained bitumen and salt from the Dead Sea for trade.

Diodorus Siculus, who wrote about 60 BC, tells of people living along the shores of the Red Sea, where they dwelt in caves. He describes many other barbarian tribes, some of them quite primitive. Thus we see that both low and high types of humanity lived together at that time. We have no good reason for concluding that the less advanced people were in any way ancestors of the cultured ones.

A review of all these facts makes it plain that immediately after the Flood, while the rivers of the world were cutting down their channels to the present levels, the earth witnessed a widespread distribution of Neanderthal and related types of humanity around the fringes of civilization. Some of them deteriorated almost to the level of the animals. But as others followed, and living conditions improved, mankind progressed in the making of tools and in the construction of dwellings.

It is equally evident that the great cities of the Mediterranean lands, of Mesopotamia, of Egypt, began with a high degree of civilization. They did not come up through a series of evolutionary cultures. Believers in the Biblical chronology have nothing to fear from the discoveries of the archaeologists.

Recapitulation

Now that we have covered the various lines of evidence for Creation and the Flood, the reader may well inquire, "Well, now what has been proved?"

Nothing, actually. We can neither prove nor disprove evolution—and the same applies to Creation. All that we can do is to assemble the data bearing on such questions and arrange the facts around a *model*.

The evolution model holds that the earth was formed from primordial matter by natural processes, that life arose spontaneously, that plants and animals have arisen through natural development, and that man has descended from animal ancestry. Correlated with such assumptions is the theory that normal geological activity laid the fossils down during long ages of time.

The Creation model—as used in this book—holds that in the beginning God created the earth and its life, including man, by special creative acts different from anything now going on, and that after He finished Creation, He has maintained the earth and its life by His divine power. The Flood described in Genesis largely buried the fossils.

120

Recapitulation

The purpose of this book has been to show how scientific data can apply with as equal validity to the Creation-Flood model as to the evolution model, and as may believe, more effectually. Consequently, what have we observed in the various fields of evidence?

From the beginning of the historical record man has put forward two major premises to explain the origin of the earth and its life. The naturalistic, or evolutionary, view has been that the earth came from primordial matter and that its features developed through the agency of inherent potentialities. Likewise, all living things arose by the action of natural inherent forces. Man has an animal origin. All the steps took place during millions of years of evolutionary development. The Flood story of Genesis is either a tale of a local catastrophe or only a religious myth.

But we have shown that humanity must also examine another interpretation. If the Genesis record of Creation and the Flood is an inspired historical record, it contains no room in it for long ages of evolution. Therefore we must consider direct Creation and a universal flood as an alternative to the popular theory of evolutionary geology.

When modern biological science first arose, a major question was the definition of species and how they formed. Linnaeus, who developed the system of classification, taught that species were fixed, and had made no change since Creation. But a hundred years later Darwin's theory of natural selection led the world to accept evolution. Then at the beginning of the twentieth century, a revolt began against evolution, and it has continued to have an influence.

121

New Creationism

Austin H. Clark, a renowned scientist connected with the National Museum in Washington, D.C., declared that all major groups of animals have remained unchanged through all past time, but within the major groups, constant and continual change has occurred. It led to the distinction between microevolution and macroevolution.

Creationists can accept the idea of microevolution, which explains by known genetic processes how genera and species could have arisen from the original created types. But they maintain that we have yet to find any proof for macroevolution—the appearance of the major groups by natural processes. The major groups—families and higher categories—show no evidence of basic change whatsoever. In the past twenty years our knowledge about the nature of genes has increased tremendously, especially in the area of DNA, the chemical component of the genes. We now know the complex nucleic acid to be so elaborately constructed that there seems to be no possible chance it could have originated by any natural processes.

Equally vital evidence has accumulated in the field of geology to support the Creation-Flood model. Fossils give evidence of rapid burial, and many rocks give indication of having formed under catastrophic conditions. One can just as effectively explain the sequence of the fossils in the rocks as burial of ancient life zones as of successive ages of time. The theory of Ecological Zonation offers an alternative to the geological ages theory.

Recent discoveries of fossil man or of hominids—manlike creatures—have thrown anthropology into a state of perplexity. They have made it necessary to revise all former theories about man's ancestry, and many facts recently brought to light make the theory of man's animal ancestry practically untenable.

Excavations and explorations in the Middle East and nearby areas have focused new light on the origin of civilization, and it is not favorable to the evolutionary interpretation. Careful evaluation of the evidence leads the believer in the Bible to be more confident than ever that he can accept the record of the Flood rather than the theory of slow advancement of primitive man through long ages.

All in all, the present situation is one of great interest and gives the creationist who literally accepts the Genesis record great confidence in the validity of his position.

Recommended Readings on Creation

Books on evolution are available at any library, but books on Creation are not so easily obtainable. For the benefit of those who wish to investigate further, I list a few books on the basic principles of creationism. I might give many more, but I have found these to be dependable discussions of the problems of evolution versus Creation. The authors may not fully agree on all points, but they are in harmony on major principles.

You may obtain the books from the publishers or from any Adventist Book Center.

Clark, Harold W. *Battle Over Genesis*. A history of evolution versus creationism. Review & Herald, Takoma Park, Washington, D.C. 20012.

————*Fossils, Flood, and Fire*. The only book in print that makes an attempt to trace the rocks in terms of the sequence of events during the Flood. Outdoor Pictures.

Clark, Robert E. D. *God Beyond Nature*. Pacific Press, Mountain View, California 94020.

Marsh, Frank L. *Evolution, Creation, and Science*. Review & Herald.

————*Life, Man, and Time*. Outdoor Pictures.

Recommended Readings on Creation

————*Variation and Fixity in Nature.* The best treatise available on the problem of the origin of species. Pacific Press.

Morris, Henry M. You may obtain Morris' books from Creation-Life Publishers,* Box 15666, San Diego, California 92115.

————*The Genesis Flood.* On a college level. It is a powerful argument for both the scientific and Biblical aspects of the Flood.

————*Scientific Creationism.* A resource handbook, especially for teachers, but the general reader will find it highly informational. I recommend the Public School Edition, as it deals only with the scientific aspects of the question.

————*The Troubled Waters of Evolution.* A valuable reference on the historical and cultural aspects of evolution.

✓Ritland, Richard M. *Search for Meaning in Nature.* An evaluation of science in the light of the validity of creationism. Pacific Press.

Utt, Richard, ed. *Creation, Nature's Designs and Designer.* Pacific Press

Wheeler, Gerald. *The Two-Taled Dinosaur.* Historical and philosophical aspects of evolution and Creation. Southern Publishing Association, Nashville, Tennessee 37202.

————————

*Creation-Life Publishers publish many other books on creationism. Write for information.

Journal Publications

The Creation Research Society publishes a quarterly and annual journal. Membership is open to anyone who holds a degree of MA or higher in natural science and who declares his belief in the Creation record in Genesis. Nonmembers may subscribe. Remit to the membership secretary, Wilbert H. Rusch, Sr., 2717 Cranbrook Road, Ann Arbor, Michigan 48104.

The Bible-Science Association publishes a monthly newsletter. Box 6131, Minneapolis, Minnesota 55406.

Origins is a publication of the Geoscience Research Institute. About 50 pages, twice a year. Loma Linda, California 92354.

Filmstrips and Tapes

Evolution and the Bible. Eight filmstrips with script or tape. Price depends on whether you order script or tape. Review & Herald.

Fundamental Creationism. A series of ten cassette tapes covering all aspects of Creation and the Flood. Outdoor Pictures, Box 277, Anacortes, Washington 98221.

Index

Flood, The Genesis, by
  Morris   19
Fossils   14, 68, 73ff
Fossils, Flood, and Fire, by
  Clark   19

Galápagos Islands   21, 22
Gene, theory of   32, 41, 42
Genesis Flood   19
Genetic code   41, 47, 48
Geologic Time Scale   56-58
Geology, Deluge or Flood   17,
  55, 82
Geoscience Research In-
  stitute   18
Glaciation   91ff, 98, 109
Goldschmidt, Richard   37, 38,
  43
Great Chain of Being   97

Hawaii, birds of   26
Heredity   20
Hutton, James   15
Huxley   16, 24
Hybridization   30

Igneous rocks   88ff
Iron Age   111

Lamarck, Jean Baptiste   14
Leakey, Louis and Mary   101
  Richard   103
Life, origin of   51
Linnaeus, Charles   12, 25, 120
Lyell, Charles   13, 21

Macroevolution   38, 49, 50,
  122
Man, origin of   98ff
Mendel, Gregor   29ff
Microevolution   38, 53

Middle East, settlement
  of   116, 123
Morgan, Thomas Hunt   32, 36
Morris, Henry M.   19
Mutation   43

Naturalism   121
Natural selection   16, 29,
  34-37, 53, 121
Nature worship   9
Neanderthal man   98, 106, 114

Origin of species   23, 42ff, 52

Paleolithic man   113
Philosophy, Arabian   11
  Greek   9
Pithecanthropus   100
Preadaptation   44, 47, 53
Price, George McCready   16

Radioactive dating   59ff
Ramapithecus   104
Reformation and Creation   12
Rift Valley of Africa   83

Smith, William   56
Species, definition of   25
  desert types   25
  origin of new   28, 32ff, 46, 52,
  53
Spontaneous generation   51
Stone Age   111

Tree-ring dating   62ff

Uranium dating   38

Variation   26, 29, 33, 37, 40,
  45, 46